THE YOUNG REBEL
IN AMERICAN LITERATURE

Edited by Carl Bode

THE FOLCROFT PRESS INC. /1970

THE YOUNG REBEL
IN AMERICAN LITERATURE

Edited by Carl Bode

FREDERICK A. PRAEGER, *Publishers*

NEW YORK

BOOKS THAT MATTER
Published in the United States of America in 1960
by Frederick A. Praeger, Inc., Publishers
64 University Place, New York 3, N. Y.

© 1959 by Carl Bode
Library of Congress catalog card number 60-12700

THE YOUNG REBEL IN AMERICAN LITERATURE
is published in two editions:
A Praeger Paperback (PPS-28)
A clothbound edition

Manufactured in the United States of America

CONTENTS

ACKNOWLEDGMENTS

Grateful acknowledgments are due to the following for permission to quote from works in copyright:

Harcourt, Brace & Co., publishers of *Free Air* and *Babbitt* by Sinclair Lewis; Mrs. Frances Scott Fitzgerald Lanahan for *This Side of Paradise* by F. Scott Fitzgerald; the author and the *Saturday Review* for "H. L. Mencken at Seventy-Five" by William Manchester; The Viking Press, publishers of *The Grapes of Wrath* and *East of Eden* by John Steinbeck; Harper & Brothers, publishers of *You Can't Go Home Again* by Thomas Wolfe; and Random House, publishers of *As I Lay Dying, Requiem for a Nun,* and *A Fable* by William Faulkner.

A WORD OF EXPLANATION

THE ASSERTIONS THAT THIS IS AN AGE OF CONFORMITY are so frequent and the evidences cited so numerous that they ought to be taken seriously. However, it is worth reminding ourselves that there is a vigorous American tradition of nonconformity, of dissent and criticism, as well. Certainly the literary heritage has not been a tame one. Both in the lives of American authors and in their works the evidences of rebellion are ample.

It was this tradition of protest that was chosen as the unifying theme for the first series of lectures on American literature ever presented at the American Embassy in London. All the lecturers were specialists in American literature. Five were themselves American—four of them on Fulbright appointments, the fifth the current Cultural Attaché in the Embassy. Of the two British lecturers, one was a member of the teaching staff of the University of Manchester, the other a senior Lecturer and Fellow at Cambridge. Their methods of attack were various. Each lecturer interpreted his broad assignment in his own terms. These ranged from a general critical appraisal to a strict attempt to establish the rebellion in the work and in the man under consideration.

So enthusiastic was the response to these seven lectures—standing-room-only attendance, and subsequent requests from editors of literary magazines for permission to publish portions of the series—that it was decided they should be assembled in book form and made available to a wider audience of Americans as well as British. All the lectures are reprinted here substantially as they were given. It is hoped that they will show the general reader a vital element in American literature.

C.B.
University of Maryland
March, 1960

THOREAU:
THE DOUBLE NEGATIVE

BY CARL BODE

W E MUST BE REALISTIC ABOUT THIS. VIEWED FROM A distant land, the American character appears simple and not always pleasing. The United States is a country of materialism and conformity, the foreign student will probably assert. He will quote—selectively—from newspaper, radio, television, and film to illustrate his point. He will have heard that much research on the nature of American society concentrates on conformity. It is the 'organisation man' rather than the individualist who is now being studied. What the foreign student will probably not know is that patterns of materialism and conformity—which do indeed exist—are by no means the only patterns. They are far from telling the whole story.

The transatlantic view of American literature is equally simple, though somewhat less forbidding. Nearly all American writing of distinction before the nineteenth century is unknown outside of the United States. The names of the most noted of our early authors may evoke a nod from the overseas reader, it is true, but it will be for reasons less than literary. Benjamin Franklin, to cite the best example, will be recognised as a statesman and scientist rather than as a writer. The fact that Washington Irving is known to have written some tales and Fenimore Cooper to have invented the fictional Indian is not very significant.

Only when we come to the New England Transcendentalists—and Emerson and Thoreau in particular—

3

in the second quarter of the nineteenth century, will we encounter American writers who now enjoy an international reputation. From that time onwards, however, the foreign student can read the roll, even at a distance, of one great name after another, from Hawthorne, Whitman, and Melville down to Frost, Hemingway, and Faulkner.

What the reader will not be apt to realise is that the very writers whose names he knows, and some of whose works he may have read, represent a tradition of anti-materialism and nonconformity. In their lives as well as their works they often stood for idealism and revolt. As a matter of fact, most of the American writers honoured by their countrymen today were rebels. They were, moreover, active critics of precisely the aspects of American life which foreign readers find least appealing. In those writers both idealism and revolt appear, but revolt is dominant. To illustrate the differing manifestations of it in our literature, we might examine Thoreau, Whitman, Sinclair Lewis, Scott Fitzgerald, Mencken, Steinbeck, and Faulkner. In some the rebellion will be more prominent than in others. In some it will show in the personal life more than in the literary work. But it will be manifest in all.

By examining these writers we should be able to see a side of American culture that is surprisingly new and fresh to many a foreign reader. Our main interest here, however, is much more literary than cultural in the sociological sense. That means that rebellion is not enough. It must be rebellion as embodied in outstanding literature.

Suppose we begin, then, with the writer Henry David

Thoreau, of Concord, Mass., who was born (squalling indignantly, no doubt) in 1817 and who died (peacefully, it has been testified) in 1862. What different things distinguish him and his work?

The first has less to do with rebellion than with literature—and more to do with tradition than with revolt. It is that he went on after graduation from Harvard College to become perhaps the best classicist of his time. The library he accumulated was remarkable and the use he made of it was great. He drew often from the literatures of both Greece and Rome. The most obvious way was through quotation and allusion. But he also composed translations from the classics, especially in the early years of his career. The outstanding example is certainly the fine set of translations from Anacreon that he made during his twenties. His reading of the classics influenced his style and accounted at least in part for its felicity. And, in addition, it may be hazarded that Greek and Roman literature contributed to a tone in his writing and to a poise of mind that could themselves justly be called classical.

His classicism is perhaps the central element in Thoreau's writing. It is the custom to place him in the romantic movement in America, but his affiliations were more with Greece and Rome than with Wordsworth or Coleridge. Regardless of his affiliations he made himself into a major artist and gave us at least one unique book. Later we shall cite some examples of his literary art, though space will allow only a few. In the meantime, it may be enough to observe that the chief justification for studying Thoreau is the obvious one: he was, simply, a great writer. Here, however, we are focusing on his rebellion. And that is to be found most notably in his ideas.

No one can separate what a man is saying from how he says it; yet it is a fair guess that Thoreau's ideas rather than his style influenced such persons as Keir Hardie, the founder of the British Labour movement. The same holds true for Thoreau's most noted reader, Mahatma Gandhi. He was given a copy of Thoreau's essay *Civil Disobedience*, first printed in 1849, during his early struggles in South Africa. "It left a deep impression upon me," he observed. He took it with him when he travelled; he read it when he was in prison.

Thoreau's ideas continue to have influence. Today his views seem to appeal to many an average man if not to his leaders. Indeed, as a minority report if nothing else, the ideas in *Civil Disobedience* and *Walden* grow in significance. They are far harder to dismiss now than they were a century ago. They have acquired an "awkward credibility" (to use the phrase of one biographer) which not only helps to keep his fame alive but increases it. The best tangible evidence of Thoreau's standing in England is that British publishers issued three separate editions of *Walden* in one recent year, 1955. Admittedly, to read a book is not necessarily to be influenced by it; yet the fact of those three editions cannot be ignored.

To see his ideas develop, we might begin by looking at Thoreau when he reached twenty—a very good age for rebellion.

He had just graduated from Harvard College and come

home to Concord. He had taken a reasonably good degree, not outstanding but good enough. He had already written a little. He had been exposed to one of the notable teachers of English of that day, Edward Tyrrell Channing; and Channing had tried to teach him unity, coherence, and emphasis, those three gods of the teacher of composition. The result was far from good, however. It took him ten years to recover from Channing's influence and become his own man. It required that length of time to eliminate the unity, coherence, and emphasis that Channing liked and replace it with Thoreau's individual mode.

Otherwise Thoreau at twenty seemed fairly well equipped for life. Physically, he was rather short, but he had a long stride. His face was distinguished by a drooping nose and liquid eye, an eye which did not like to look at other people. He was healthy and a person of marvellous physical organisation. Emerson says that when Thoreau got to his pencil-making days he could take a box of pencils, reach in, and grasp exactly a dozen each time. That kind of physical fineness long remained a factor in Thoreau's sensory appreciation of nature and indeed in his passion for it.

Young Thoreau's psychological make-up was, on the surface, rather ordinary. He had been a bit rebellious in college, but that was to be expected. This was a Harvard of a lustier period than today, a Harvard of the time when no decent girl (the town gossips averred) could be seen strolling on the campus without risk to her reputation. This was the heyday of student riots. One during

Thoreau's time is especially memorable. The boys dismembered the furniture, threw it out the windows, and then built a bonfire of it in the courtyard. A tutor who tried to restore order was repelled, as Thoreau reported in a lively letter, by loud threats to "saw his leg off" and do other terrifying things. That kind of rebellion was general. Thoreau also rebelled on occasion against Harvard's moralism, but in this he found fewer companions.

His greatest problem at twenty was that, somehow or other, he had got the idea that he ought to become a poet —and make poetry his life and his living. He meant, moreover, to be a poet not only as a writer of rhymes but as a prophet, acting, if you will, as a seer. This was a high and transcendental ambition. In Thoreau it was to persist for years, despite the fact that America has always treated her poets just as shabbily as any other country. His problem of a century ago was if anything more acute than it would be today. His struggles in the attempt to solve it were the typical ones—with the single notable exception to be analysed later.

He began by looking for a school. Teaching remains the prime refuge of the poet and Thoreau tried, erratically, to become a schoolmaster. He made the mistake of agreeing to teach at his local school in Concord. A member of the school committee who knew him well came by one day and suggested that more discipline was in order. Thoreau indignantly caned every child in the school. Then he dismissed them all and quit his job. Thereafter he did only a little more teaching, though he tried more than once to find a suitable post. He applied as far away, in fact, as Kentucky, but he was not successful.

Next he did what most American writers do today. He went to New York to try and crack the literary market. His friend Ralph Waldo Emerson arranged the means. He had a brother with a rather dull son and Thoreau was commissioned to tutor the son. The family lived in Staten Island, which is just a short distance from New York City. Riding out from Staten Island, Thoreau began to make the rounds of the publishing houses. He had no success. Here and there editors hinted that if he had something popular rather than quaint they might be interested in it. But that was all.

When he returned from Staten Island to Concord, his difficulties increased. Back home again, he passed the neighbours who pointed out that here was a Harvard graduate (in a day when that was a great rarity) and asked what was he doing with his life. The answer seemed to be, nothing. He was merely an idler, a vagabond. Now even his family felt defensive about him. They were on his side, yet they would have been less than human if they had not at times looked rather sadly at Henry and wondered when he was going to straighten out. He did a little work, odd jobs here and there, but nothing that he cared for; later on he would do some pencil-making and surveying. Ultimately he would go into the production of graphite and sell enough of that to earn a living. But for young Thoreau there was still the basic problem of being a poet and staying alive.

He was near thirty when he found an answer and decided on his most famous action. It was during the year 1845 that he decided to go to Walden Pond. There he built a cabin, the most famous one in American literature, and there he established his life with a minimum of labour. He cultivated a patch of beans and he grew a few other vegetables. The rest of the time he either sauntered around the countryside—and it was a very beautiful one at the time—or else he wrote. When he wanted to, he came home at week-ends. This was no Robinson Crusoe existence, it should be added. Thoreau did not intend to prove that he could exist independently. He wanted to prove that he could find out what life was like and also find enough time to write about it.

In the two years that he spent at Walden—and he went on 4th July, Independence Day—he wrote his first book, called *A Week on the Concord and Merrimack Rivers*. The *Week* proved to be an imperfect, badly-structured, but in many ways original work. It was a combination of travel, history, and observation, with some college essays and philosophising stuffed in here and there out of youthful economy.

More important, it was at Walden Pond that he did most of the first draft of *Walden* itself (though the book did not come out till 1854). And he laboured on it. The manuscripts of that draft can be seen at the Huntington Library in California. Lines are crossed out, paragraphs are rearranged, words are inserted, all indicating the care and trouble he took to get his final effect of classical ease. It is the more remarkable because this was a time when the prose of the typical American writer was much too full-blown.

Thoreau: The Double Negative

This sojourn at Walden was a remarkable experience. It remained in many ways the high point of his creative life. After he left Walden, he went downhill both as a writer and as a Transcendentalist, though his descent was always a gradual one; yet it dates from the sleepy day in September 1847 when he became bored and returned to Concord.

Of course he continued to do some writing after the Walden period. He wrote, however, more and more as a naturalist and less as the Transcendentalist one finds in *Walden*. He became almost a nature diarist, though an excellent one; the poet largely disappeared. But the diarist was Thoreau in his late thirties and early forties, and he does not concern us here. We are concerned instead especially with young Thoreau the rebel, and the nature of his revolt, both negative and positive.

We turn now, in other words, to the anatomy of Thoreau's rebellion.

On the negative side he was a 'protestant'. He protested against many things. One of the most telling comments about this fact was made by Emerson in a brilliant short life of Thoreau which developed from the eulogy that Emerson prepared after Thoreau's death. Emerson has this to say: "There was somewhat military in his nature, not to be subdued, always manly and able, but rarely tender, as if he did not feel himself except in opposition." It would be hard to find a better rendering of Thoreau the rebel than that: "he did not feel himself except in opposition".

A characteristic aspect of his 'protestantism' was the

animosity he felt towards both his peers and the older generation. And it was a genuine animosity. It was something emotional as well as intellectual. Underlying it was Thoreau's deepening conviction that his ideas about value were superior to those of anyone around him but especially to those of his elders. He summed it up with whimsical irony in a famous passage from *Walden*: "The greater part of what my neighbours call good, I believe in my soul to be bad, and if I repent of anything, it is very likely to be my good behaviour. What demon possessed me that I behaved so well? You may say the wisest thing you can, old man—you who have lived seventy years, not without honour of a kind—I hear an irresistible voice which invites me away from all that. One generation abandons the enterprises of another like stranded vessels."

In political matters his 'protestantism' stood out. He denied the basic premise of democracy in America, the belief in majority rule. He questioned the wisdom of the majority and rejected its claim to impose on the minority. As he asserted in *Civil Disobedience*, the majority was never necessarily right or necessarily fair to the minority. In fact, he implied that the contrary was true. Brute power alone allowed the majority to carry out its desires. Others in America also criticised majority rule at this time, particularly Southern political leaders in the debate on slavery; but no one went as far as Thoreau. In almost every situation he was a minority man.

The State personified the will of the majority, and it was against the State that Thoreau soon rebelled. His protest began quietly, increased in vigour, was climaxed by a night in prison, and then diminished in the last few years of his life because the State let him alone. And, ironically, one of the reasons that the State finally let him alone was that they both reached the same conclusion— though by different paths—that slavery had to be fought with force.

But in the years before the start of the Civil War there were two things that Thoreau rebelled against most earnestly, two things that struck him as being the grossest of wrongs committed by the government. One was the participation of the United States in the Mexican-American War of 1846. To Thoreau this was a war of imperialism. It was a war which had no ethical reason for it whatsoever and he thought that it should be opposed in every way. The other was the government position in the middle 1840s and the 1850s on slavery. Local and national government stood on the same side. Massachusetts itself—Thoreau's own State—not only countenanced the legal aspects of slavery but co-operated in returning escaped slaves to the South. The Federal Government took the position that slavery was protected by the law and consequently must be upheld and defended to the extent that the law allowed.

Thoreau's protest against slavery was, to begin with, based on principle only. It was not motivated by zeal or by simple humanitarianism. We can see that, when he says sharply that many abolitionists are fools and busybodies. They try to reform Negro slavery when they should start instead by reforming themselves. They lie

13

enchained by prejudice, by ignorance, by stupidity. Let them pay attention to freeing themselves first and then fare South to free the Negro slave.

However, as time went on he grew interested in, and then devoted to, the abolitionist movement itself. Towards the end of his life, he met the man who concluded his conversion. That was the militant abolitionist John Brown. Thoreau's most burning essays are dedicated to Brown's defence. By the time he met Brown, Thoreau himself was part of the underground railroad as an active abolitionist. But this was Thoreau in middle age. The early Thoreau had the feeling that reform, like charity, might well begin at home and begin with the individual rather than the group. Furthermore, he did not feel that he ought to be what is called in American political slang 'a bleeding heart'. He said in *Civil Disobedience*: "It is not a man's duty, as a matter of course, to devote himself to the eradication of any, even the most enormous, wrong; he may still properly have other concerns to engage him; but it is his duty, at least, to wash his hands of it." Thoreau suited the action to the word. He decided that if he was paying taxes or exercising any of his political rights, then he was involved in the State. And his duty was to disengage himself. As a matter of fact, he even issued a document, edged with irony, stating that "I, Henry Thoreau, do not wish to be regarded as a member of any incorporated society which I have not joined".

The crucial issue was raised when Thoreau refused to pay his poll tax. He would pay his local road tax because he wanted to be a good neighbour, but not the State's poll tax. Finally Sam Staples, the Concord gaoler, hailed him in and put him into prison; there, after he was introduced around, he settled for the night. He talked with some of the other inmates. He discovered that the sounds of the town heard from within the prison were very different from what they had been to him outside. The next morning he breakfasted on chocolate and brown bread. About noon, "someone interfered", said Thoreau, "and paid that tax". He was released promptly. We still do not know who paid. But suspicion falls on a maiden aunt who could not stand the disgrace of having a Thoreau in gaol. At any rate someone did pay, someone interfered, and Thoreau came out. He discovered when he emerged that people looked at him a little queerly as they passed on the street. Nevertheless, he went about his interrupted business. Before his imprisonment he had agreed to captain a huckleberry party. Now he was free again and not long afterwards he stood high on a green hill above the Concord gaol.

The foregoing can perhaps be described, without torturing terms too much, as the negative side of his rebelliousness. In his greatest personal document, *Walden*, we find the positive side as well. We find it indeed in full. And we also discover there the bridge between the negative and positive sides of the rebellion.

In *Walden*—which is basically an account of a year at Walden Pond but which is many other things beyond that—he addresses himself to two classes of people. They are those who have property and those who have not, or, to put it broadly, the rich and the poor. His rich man is the Concord landowner, the local farmer, but he stands as a symbol for the Boston merchant and the millionaire as well. This is what Thoreau says to the man of property: "I see young men, my townsmen, whose misfortune it is to have inherited farms, houses, barns, cattle, and farming tools; for these are more easily acquired than got rid of. Better if they had been born in the open pasture and suckled by a wolf, that they might have seen with clearer eyes what field they were called to labour in. Who made them serfs of the soil? Why should they eat their sixty acres, when man is condemned to eat only his peck of dirt? Why should they begin digging their graves as soon as they are born? They have got to live a man's life, pushing all these things before them, and get on as well as they can. How many a poor immortal soul have I met well nigh crushed and smothered under its load, creeping down the road of life, pushing before it a barn seventy-five feet by forty, its Augean stables never cleansed, and one hundred acres of land, tillage, mowing, pasture, and wood lot!"

Incidentally, when Thoreau arrived at Walden someone gave him a paper-weight. He discovered that it accumulated dust and that he would have to keep cleaning it if he wanted to be neat. His solution was to dispose of this little piece of property. He threw it out and kept the simple life inviolate.

This, then, is Thoreau on the man of property. But is he more sympathetic to the poor man, the man who stands in Thoreau's own shoes? Far from it. He does not consider that poverty in itself has any ennobling effect. Here is what he says as he drives home his point: "Some of you, we all know, are poor, find it hard to live, are sometimes, as it were, gasping for breath. I have no doubt that some of you who read this book are unable to pay for all the dinners which you have actually eaten, or for the coats and shoes which are fast wearing or are already worn out, and have come to this page to spend borrowed or stolen time, robbing your creditors of an hour. It is very evident what mean and sneaking lives many of you live, for my sight has been whetted by experience; always on the limits, trying to get into business and trying to get out of debt."

Thoreau rises to a climax in this passage when he turns to the sorriest of American materialists, the pitiful, petty purveyor of goods or services. He is the ancestor of Willy Loman in *Death of a Salesman* and a dozen other defeated men. And he is the man whom Thoreau apostrophises with: "Always promising to pay, promising to pay, tomorrow, and dying today, insolvent; seeking to curry favour, to get custom, by how many modes, only not state-prison offences; lying, flattering, voting, contracting yourselves into a nutshell of civility, or dilating into an atmosphere of thin and vaporous generosity, that you may persuade your neighbour to let you make his shoes, or his hat, or his coat, or his carriage, or import his groceries for him; making yourselves sick, that you may lay up something against a sick day." Probably as strong words as could be heard from an American author of that time or today.

17

These important passages from *Walden* are, for our purposes, the bridge between the negative and the positive sides of Thoreau's rebellion. He first shows what desperately useless lives both the rich and the poor are leading. This done, he shows them how to live better; and he does so through a classically artful account of his own experience.

The nature of the positive side of his rebellion is deceptively plain. Having repudiated the scale of values of his neighbours and his time, he wanted to find out what a proper scale of values should be. In this inquiry he had a cluster of questions to ask and answers to get. What is real and what is not? What is true and what is untrue? What is good and what is bad? With the questions and answers went his determination to find the way to the real, the true, and the good.

He explained his search and his intention with brilliant simplicity. Both the rich and the poor could understand it if they would. "I went to the woods," he said, "because I wished to live deliberately, to front only the essential facts of life, and to see if I could not learn what it had to teach, and not, when I came to die, discover that I had not lived. I did not wish to live what was not life, living is so dear; nor did I wish to practise resignation, unless it was quite necessary. I wanted to live deep and suck out all the marrow of life, to live so sturdily and Spartan-like as to put to rout all that was not life, to cut a broad swathe and shave close, to drive life into a corner, and reduce it to its lowest terms, and, if it proved to be mean, why then to get the whole and genuine meanness of it, and publish its meanness to the world; or if it were sublime, to know it by experience, and be able to give a true account of it in my next excursion. For most men, it appears to me, are in a strange uncertainty about it, whether it is of the Devil or of God, and have *somewhat hastily* concluded that it is the chief end of man here to 'glorify God and enjoy Him for ever'."

As these last sentences suggest, Thoreau's rebellion was against the Church as well as against the State and property. The Church stood in his scale of values. In his day Concord was said to have three religious groups. One worshipped at the Unitarian church, another worshipped at the Trinitarian church, and the third walked beside Walden Pond. If Thoreau had any shrine it was Walden. He required no others. He once remarked in a letter to a friend that he had lectured in the basement of a near-by church and had helped, he hoped, to undermine it.

To Thoreau most of American living—whether in church or street or shop—was sheer wastefulness. We were occupied with pursuits which were at the best needless and at the worst humiliating. Because we spent more time at business than anything else, business emerged as Thoreau's chief target. Perhaps nothing could give a better idea of the magnitude of what Thoreau was rebelling against than the pronouncement of an American President who came after Thoreau but stood for the same scale of values that Thoreau opposed. The President was Calvin Coolidge and he declared that "The business of this country is business". Thoreau would have hooted at that. His retort would have been that the business of this country is living, and living in terms of the most important possible things to its people. That was why, when Thoreau was offered work, was offered things to do, he usually turned them down. He talked once about a rich and stupid neighbour who wanted him to haul stones for a wall. Thoreau refused. Why should he do it? Why should he waste his time?

The whole scale of values that he found in his Concord neighbours and in the nation affronted him. He argued against it again and again, sometimes with irony, sometimes with compassion, sometimes with ardour. But he always remembered to make the general specific. He himself was often the instance for the generalisation. For example, he will speak about how a village praised a businessman who cut down its lovely forests—and yet criticised as an idler the man who wishes only to walk through them.

But Thoreau is never merely negative. He is eager to replace the values he dislikes with nobler ones. And he has a pleasantly precise recipe, one designed as much, or more, for the reader of today as for the reader of Thoreau's time. The kind of prescription that Thoreau knows how to give best will not age.

"Let us spend one day as deliberately as nature," he begins, "and not be thrown off the track by every nutshell and mosquito's wing that falls on the rails. Let us rise early and fast, or break fast gently and without perturbation; let company come and let company go; let the bells ring and the children cry——" (Thoreau was a bachelor) "—determined to make a day of it. Why should we knock under and go with the stream? Let us not be upset and overwhelmed in that terrible rapid and whirlpool called a dinner, situated in the meridian shallows. Weather this danger and you are safe, for the rest of the way is down hill. With unrelaxed nerves, with morning vigour, sail by it, looking another way, tied to the mast like Ulysses. If the engine whistles, let it whistle, till it is hoarse for its pains. If the bell rings, why should we run? We will consider what kind of music they are like."

And here is the salient sentence in this section of *Walden*: "Let us settle ourselves and work and wedge our feet downward through the mud and slush of opinion, and prejudice, and tradition, and delusion, and appearance, the alluvium which covers the globe, through Paris and London, through New York and Boston and Concord, through church and state, through poetry and philosophy and religion, till we come to a hard bottom and rocks in place, which we can call *reality*, and say: 'This is.'"

Once reality has been found, a life can be built upon it. Thoreau believes that when we discover what is real, we can determine what is good and true. After the rebellion has been successful a new life can begin. This is what he suggests in the conclusion to *Walden*. The promise he holds out there to his reader is one of the most memorable in American letters. "If one advances confidently in the direction of his dreams, and endeavours to live the life which he has imagined, he will meet with a success unexpected in common hours. He will put some things behind, will pass an invisible boundary; new, universal, and more liberal laws will begin to establish themselves around and within him; or the old laws be expanded, and interpreted in his favour in a more liberal sense, and he will live with a licence of a higher order of beings."

In these lines Thoreau saves for the last his most important instruction, one that is surely even more useful today than when *Walden* was written. "The gift to be simple" the Shakers in America called it when Thoreau was alive. He puts it this way to his reader: "In proportion as he simplifies his life, the laws of the universe will appear less complex, and solitude will not be solitude, nor poverty poverty, nor weakness weakness. If you have built castles in the air, your work need not be lost; that is where they should be. Now put the foundations under them."

WALT WHITMAN AS INNOVATOR

BY DAVID DAICHES

IF WE LOOK AT WALT WHITMAN FROM THIS SIDE OF THE Atlantic—though I have also looked at him when I was in America—we can get a perspective which may be enlightening and perhaps somewhat different from the perspective one gets from looking at and reading Whitman in his native habitat.

'Young rebel' is not of course the term to apply to old Walt. You must be familiar with portraits and photographs of him, whether the later ones with a long white prophetic beard or the early one that appeared in the 1855 edition of *Leaves of Grass*, with one hand on hip and the other in pocket, laughing to himself. 'Young' does not quite suit either case. He was thirty-six when *Leaves of Grass* was first published and he spent the rest of his life re-writing it, building it up into a great poetic autobiography so that, as he wrote later: "This is no book; Who touches this, touches a man."

Was he a rebel and if so in what respect? What kind of rebel? How good a rebel? How fruitful a rebel? And in what direction? The question is complicated by the extraordinary legends that have grown up around Whitman and which were fostered by Whitman himself. Ever a poseur, he tried to act out certain kinds of poetic character which he thought would assist the proper appreciation of his poems, and one of the several roles he liked to act was that of the free, healthy, hearty, independent American tough. That role is the one, I think, that he is most popularly known by. We think of Whitman as the great optimistic affirmer of democratic hope, of new-world expansiveness and optimism and progress, with his eyes glancing all over the enormous American continent, making tremendous play with the picturesque place-names, north and south and east and west; projecting himself with great 'thundering speech' all over the United States in a wide gesture of embracing, of affirming, of life, of optimism, and of general 'O-kayness'.

Recently there have been attempts made to reverse that traditional picture of Whitman. In a recent essay Leslie Fiedler has suggested that the Whitman we really appreciate today is not the optimistic affirmer of American prospects but the tortured, ambivalent, complex invalid whose greatest poems always contained a death-wish. I do not think that will quite do. I do not think you can simply turn the tradition upside-down and say that the true Whitman is not the optimistic affirmer but the negative denier. I am inclined to believe that Richard Chase's recent study of Whitman, which I think is the best short study there is, reconsiders Whitman more effectively than Fiedler does and takes account of the elegiac aspect of his poetry, while at the same time relating it to, seeing it in a fruitful counterpoint against, his more traditional, optimistic, expansive side. Mr. Chase sees Whitman as a comic poet and as an elegiac poet and he sees these two elements as somehow related to each other and arising out of each other. I do not want to pursue his ingenious and subtle argument on this point; I want only to suggest that it is a fruitful new approach to Whitman, and one that will have most effect on modern criticism.

I would like myself, however, to consider more strictly the terms of the title of this series—the young rebel. Leaving out the 'young', let me ask: how was Whitman a rebel, and why was he a rebel, and to what end was he a rebel? By rebel I simply mean someone who is against the established way of doing things and is trying to do them in a new way, and not only new, but more interesting, more workable, more lively, more fruitful. I think the best approach to this question is in terms of what Mr. Eliot has called "tradition and the individual talent". I think perhaps it can be said that Whitman's primary contribution as an innovator in literature was to offer new solutions to the problems posed by the relation between tradition and the individual talent. It has always been a problem; perhaps—as anyone who has wrestled with trying to write creatively must know—perhaps the greatest of all artistic problems: how the individual can come to terms with the general postulates about art which his culture provides him with; and also in a larger sense how individual experience can come to terms with contemporary religious or philosophical or social tradition. There is inevitably a dichotomy, a gap, between your own æsthetic experience and the lessons you learn from it and what you learn from the pulpit and the platform.

The more traditional English or European way of handling this problem has been a deliberate counterpointing of experience and tradition in all sorts of interesting and very often fruitful ways. If you are brought up in an age which has a strong communal belief, whether religious or philosophical or any other, you breathe it in, as it were, without perhaps examining it too closely. In any case you accept it as representing the truth about experience. If at the same time your necessarily private vision of life pushes you to express a very different vision, what are you going to do with these two different things? I can illustrate what you can do and what Whitman did not do by citing two English sonnets. One is Milton's sonnet on his blindness. Milton believed that he was destined to be a great English poet. He was stricken by blindness before he wrote his greatest work, and rebelled:

> "When I consider how my light is spent,
>   Ere half my days, in this dark world and wide,
>   And that one Talent which is death to hide,
>   Lodg'd with me useless . . ."

He murmured and complained, but then he set his complaint against the Christian tradition which he believed in; God knew what He was doing, and the poem ends in resignation and patience and hope. "They also serve who only stand and waite."

Milton makes a similar point in his great lament for his dead friend in 'Lycidas' when he says in effect: What is the use of going on if you are liable to be cut off by sudden death; what is the use of preparing yourself to be a great writer? The answer is: Never mind, God knows what He is doing; we will carry on as long as we are alive, "Tomorrow to fresh Woods, and Pastures new." In his counterpointing of personal experience and tradition he had closed the gap between the two. It is across that gap that the poetic vision sparks. That is how the great European poets of the past very often operated. That is how Dante operated, and Milton, and the great Greek dramatists—they pitted a personal vision against the traditional mythology of their people. And, as I say, across the gap you get the spark of literature.

Now, when public belief becomes less insistent in its demands, when it becomes less stable and certain (as it did in the nineteenth century), the poet has no longer the two clear poles of traditional formulation and personal experience between which his sensibility must move and which he has to come to terms with simultaneously. He turns instead to the one pole, the self, the introspective self. When Keats reflects, as Milton had reflected, that he could die before writing his best poetry, he does not end by coming to terms with religion. He does not say, God knows what He is doing, "Tomorrow to fresh Woods, and Pastures new." He turns instead to sheer elegiac introspection.

> "When I have fears that I may cease to be
> Before my pen has glean'd my teeming brain"—

when he is afraid that he may die before he has written what it is in him to write:

> ". . . then on the shore
> Of the wide world I stand alone, and think,
> Till Love and Fame to nothingness do sink."

That tendency to elegiac introspection develops in a literature when the pole of traditional affirmation is missing and the poet is forced back solely on his personal experience. All the great nineteenth-century poets of England found themselves at their most characteristic moments walking plangently by the sea—Matthew Arnold in 'Dover Beach', Tennyson in 'Break, Break, Break', for instance. It is the traditional elegiac mode of Victorian poetry.

Now this is where I think we can see quite precisely the novelty, the rebelliousness if you like, of Whitman. In the Victorian elegiac mode, in Tennyson and Arnold and so many others, the poet broods in a scene which is set in order to deflect all attention back to the self. The sea in Arnold's 'Dover Beach' does not make Arnold lift his eyes to wonder about what other shores it may be lapping but pushes him back to himself and the little society which he has built up against the ruins. "Let us be true to one another"—because there is nothing else left in life. And the evidence of ordinary people going about their business in Tennyson's 'Break, Break, Break', the commerce of the world going on—"And the stately ships go on To their haven under the hill"—only increases the sense of the poet's self-regarding woe. "O well for the fisherman's boy, that he shouts with his sister at play!"—but as for the poet, he is longing for "the touch of a vanish'd hand". The external world is simply a scene set in order to deflect the poet's attention to the unhappiness of his own plangent situation.

There are three factors involved here—first, the self;

secondly, the setting; and thirdly, the art, the available
literary forms. If we move from 'Break, Break, Break'
or Arnold's 'Dover Beach', which is a song of himself, to
Whitman's 'Song of Myself', we see at once a radically
different orientation of the poet with respect to himself,
to the physical setting, and to the traditional artfulness
which he employs. You will remember, those of you
who know Whitman at all, the little inscription among
the many introductory inscriptions he added to his poems
—'One's-Self I Sing':

> "One's-self I sing, a simple separate person,
> Yet utter the word Democratic, the word En-Masse."

'One's-self I sing' not 'myself I sing'. 'One' is an inter-
mediate pronoun between 'me' and 'you'; it is the im-
personalising of the self immediately—the very first word.
You cannot imagine Arnold or Tennyson using the word
'one' to refer to themselves either in 'Dover Beach' or in
'In Memoriam' or anywhere else.
   Consider Whitman's opening:

> "I celebrate myself, and sing myself,
>   And what I assume you shall assume,
>   For every atom belonging to me as good
>   belongs to you."

The colloquialness, the ease of speech, is one thing. This
poet's relation to traditional artfulness is obviously
different from Tennyson's or Arnold's, but his attitude

to himself is also somewhat different. In spite of the driving egotism, the self is somehow transmuted from the beginning, as it is in the first word of the opening inscription, 'One's-self I sing'. Whitman is concerned to build up in his own special way a picture of the relationship of his self, first to other selves, secondly to the external world of nature, and thirdly to other moments in time than the moment which he is experiencing now. There is both a spatial and a temporal relationship developed here. The relationship of the poet to external nature is not one simply of a poet who gets from nature certain scenic assistance, as though nature is the great backdrop for human emotion. Whitman is different. Exactly how different will emerge as I take up one or two quotations and try and put them in this context of my present discussion, trying to differentiate between the normal English nineteenth-century way of handling these problems and Whitman's way.

> "There never was any more inception than there is
>   now,
> Nor any more youth or age than there is now,
> And will never be any more perfection than there is
>   now,
> Nor any more heaven or hell than there is now."

That almost incantatory and repetitive statement that occurs at another point in 'Song of Myself' is another clue to Whitman's handling of the whole problem of the relationship of the self at the present moment to the self at other moments in history, in time.

One or two more quotations before I explain myself
further, still from 'Song of Myself'.

"Trippers and askers surround me,
    People I meet, the effect upon me of my early
        life or the ward and city I live in, or the
        nation,
    The latest dates, discoveries, inventions, societies,
        authors old and new,
    My dinner, dress, associates, looks, compliments, dues,
    The real or fancied indifference of some man or
        woman I love,
    The sickness of one of my folks or of myself, or ill-
        doing or loss or lack of money, or depressions or
        exaltations,
    Battles, the horrors of fratricidal war, the fever of
        doubtful news, the fitful events;
    These come to me days and nights and go from me
        again,
    But they are not the Me myself.

Apart from the pulling and hauling stands what I am,
Stands amused, complacent, compassionating, idle,
    unitary,
Looks down, is erect, or bends an arm on an impalp-
    able certain rest,
Looking with side-curved head curious what will
    come next,
Both in and out of the game and watching and
    wondering at it."

This is a most complex situation. The poet is observing other people; he is surrounded by other people—"Trippers and askers. . . . People I meet" and so on; he is concerned with daily things of life—"My dinner, dress, associates, looks, compliments, dues." At the same time that he is aware of them he is aware of his relationship with them, "But they are not the Me myself. Apart from the pulling and hauling stands what I am, Stands amused, complacent, compassionating, idle, unitary." He is cultivating deliberately a pose of awareness in the light of which his response to what he sees can be more than merely elegiac, or merely traditional, merely the report of something, merely the register of individual emotion about something.

'Song of Myself' is like so many of Whitman's poems, full of those enormous catalogues of Americana, sweeping over the country, describing its cities, sounds, scenes, in various geographical regions and professions and walks of life. These catalogues have a purpose. They are not simply there in order to build up a picture of the size or complexity or diversity of the country. They are not simply saying, as Sidney Lanier said Whitman was simply saying, that because the Mississippi is long America is great. It is not simply what most of us on this side of the Atlantic recognise as the American preoccupation with size as a good thing. It is something much more complex and interesting than that. It is an endeavour to cultivate a kind of awareness of other people so complexly developed that your own stream of consciousness while you are in the act of contemplation takes you outside of yourself and achieves a new kind of relationship between your ineradicable self (which remains the core and centre of all Whitman's poems) and the external world.

It might almost be said that Whitman is the father of that stream-of-consciousness technique which has been so popular in twentieth-century fiction. By cultivating the special kind of sensibility you can learn to depend on that sensibility. But you cannot depend on raw sensibility— or you can only if you are writing another kind of poem; it is another way of doing it. You prepare your sensibility in rather special ways. You strike certain poses, and the pose with Whitman is extremely important. It is not, as Esther Shephard tried to show in her book on Whitman's pose, something purely histrionic, although there are histrionic elements in Whitman's behaviour sometimes. This pose represents a way of chemically treating your consciousness, as it were, so that you can depend on it to register in a more than egotistical way. How can you make your stream of consciousness tell something real about the external world rather than operate only solipsistically referring back always only to yourself? That is the problem Whitman is dealing with. His aim was to make his consciousness into that sort of servant by posing it in a certain way as one poses a camera at a certain angle.

The trouble with Whitman is that to get the effect you must quote a long passage because his best effects are all cumulative, so I am afraid I have to give rather long quotations. These catalogues occur in many of the poems, but I will quote from one of the better known. He is observing the world, the American world, and identifying himself in his characteristic way with what he observes. He is—he *becomes*—the people he observes. Because his sensibility has been prepared in a certain way, he observes them in a certain way. That way is radically different from Tennyson's. In Tennyson's 'In Memoriam' the poet watches the dawn on a dull, drizzly day; the first carts rattle into the street, "the noise of life begins again". But this is just a background, against which the poet mourns over his loss. It makes Whitman, on the other hand, ask who is driving the cart, and why, and what sort of a life is there. By exploiting his experiences in this way, Whitman develops his sensibility into a kind of ideal sympathetic reporter.

"I ascend to the foretruck,
  I take my place late at night in the crow's-nest,
  We sail the arctic sea, it is plenty light enough,
  Through the clear atmosphere I stretch around on the
      wonderful beauty,
  The enormous masses of ice pass me and I pass them,
      the scenery is plain in all directions,
  The white-topt mountains show in the distance, I
      fling out my fancies toward them,

. . . .

"I am a free companion, I bivouac by invading watch-
  fires,

. . . .

"I understand the large hearts of heroes,
  The courage of present times and all times,

36

How the skipper saw the crowded and rudderless
    wreck of the steam-ship, and Death chasing it up
    and down the storm,
How he knuckled tight and gave not back an inch,
    and was faithful of days and faithful of nights,
And chalk'd in large letters on a board, Be of good
    cheer, we will not desert you;
How he follow'd with them and tack'd with them
    three days and would not give it up,
How he saved the drifting company at last,
How the lank loose-gown'd women look'd when
    boated from the side of their prepared graves,
How the silent old-faced infants and the lifted sick,
    and the sharp-lipp'd unshaven men;
All this I swallow, it tastes good, I like it well, it
    becomes mine,
I am the man, I suffer'd, I was there."

This enormous outgoing identifying power makes these
catalogues vibrant with life and interest and with more
than sympathy, because they have become part of the
poet's identity. Sympathy is a relationship between someone and someone else, but here there seems to be an actual
identity. I say 'seems' because it is not really an identity.
It is an element of sympathetic imagination working in a
special way on material which is not used simply as an
excuse for indulging the poet's original mood. It brings
the poet out of himself into new moods. That is the great
difference between the Tennysonian or Arnoldian handling of scenery or events and Whitman's handling of

scenery and events. For Whitman, what he sees becomes part of him, but in becoming part of him it changes him; he becomes a different and a more complex person. It is not simply an excuse for developing his mood. To quote from another poem, equally well known I think:

"There was a child went forth every day,
  And the first object he look'd upon, that object he
    became,
  And that object became part of him for the day or a
    certain part of the day,
  Or for many years or stretching cycles of years."

And then there is that remarkable poem 'The Sleepers' where, under the shadow of night, the poet imagines all the people who are sleeping under the different roofs of this community; and one by one he identifies himself with them in that special poetic mode which was really his invention.

Now what is all this about identifying oneself? Is this not a curious sort of sentimentality? We are ourselves; we cannot identify ourselves with other people. Well, of course we cannot—and yet in a sense we can. Whitman was very well aware of this problem and discusses it in his prose many times—the relation between identity and the sense of otherness of other people. The primary condition for the poet's sense of identity functioning in this expansive manner is that it should be a real and whole sense of identity, with no part of the poet's mind, spirit, or body suppressed. The full realisation of individuality

38

is the pre-condition for the individual's making proper contact with both his natural environment and other individuals.

"As the attributes of the poets of the Kosmos concentre in the real body and soul and in the pleasure of things, they possess the superiority of genuineness over all fiction and romance. As they emit themselves facts are showered over with light . . . the daylight is lit with more volatile light . . . also the deep between the setting and rising sun goes deeper many fold. Each precise object or condition or combination or process exhibits a beauty . . . the multiplication table its—old age its—the carpenter's trade its—the grand-opera its . . . the hugehulled cleanshaped New-York clipper at sea under steam or full sail gleams with unmatched beauty . . ." That is from the Preface to *Leaves of Grass*. It is an extraordinary thing to say. The multiplication table, old age, the carpenter's trade, grand opera (these are all out of his own experience of course; he was a great opera-goer in his youth), the New York clipper—each exhibits its own beauty so long as it remains true to its own individuating reality. The poet's duty is to both *purify* and *expand* his individual sensibility so that it can respond to and even absorb that individuating reality. This is very close indeed to Gerard Manley Hopkins's sense of quiddity; Hopkins talked about the 'thisness' of something and said that what makes a poem is its essential inward form, what he called the 'inscape'. That is very Whitmanesque, and Hopkins recognised the kinship in a rueful letter to his friend Robert Bridges when he said: "I always knew in my heart Walt Whit-

39

man's mind to be more like my own than any other man's living." He added, "As he is a very great scoundrel this is not a pleasant confession," but that is another matter. This notion that if you individualise something you also universalise it is Whitman's way of treating a problem which Hopkins treated in a similar way.

Here are one or two other significant quotations from the Preface: "The most affluent man is he that confronts all the shows he sees by equivalents out of the stronger wealth of himself." That is another way of putting T. S. Eliot's doctrine of the objective correlative. Your emotion must have some objective correlative before it can be made amenable to literary treatment. Similarly the external world must have some response in the emotion felt by the observer. "The most affluent man is he that confronts all the shows he sees by equivalents out of the stronger wealth of himself." One more quotation on this point of identity and quiddity, also from the Preface: "*Leaves of Grass* indeed (I cannot too often reiterate) has mainly been the outcropping of my own emotional and other personal nature—an attempt, from first to last, to put *a Person*, a human being (myself, in the latter half of the Nineteenth Century, in America,) freely, fully and truly on record. I could not find any similar personal record in current literature that satisfied me. But it is not on *Leaves of Grass* distinctively as *literature*, or a specimen thereof, that I feel to dwell, or advance claims. No one will get at my verses who insists upon viewing them as a literary performance, or attempt at such performance, or as aiming mainly toward art or æstheticism."

Walt Whitman as Innovator

What he is saying there is that he is hewing out his own
kind of craftsmanship in order to contain his own particular kind of personal feeling. This is a moment of
time; this individual confronts this time and it is possible,
if he cultivates the proper kind of awareness, if he trains
his sensibility, if he poses it in the proper way, to achieve
a cosmic vision which relates all time and all space to the
individual. Only by being true to one's own self can one
ever come to terms with outside reality.

I have other quotations but I must hasten on to relate
this to Whitman's view of what is real and what is bogus,
or what, in a favourite word of his, is dandified, or—to
use another favourite word—what represents charla-
tanism. Whitman's concept of dandyism (he has wonderful outbursts about the dandified young men of his day)
is much more than just sartorial or social. It refers to
prettying-up your experience so as to trim it or in some
way vitiate it. In a perceptive article on Tennyson he
pays tribute to him as a great artist and poet but says he
cannot help feeling he is dandified, that somehow the
claims of craftsmanship have interfered with his experience. Much modern criticism of Tennyson had made
just that point, though not in quite the same terms. In a
wonderful outburst against the spivs of his own day
Whitman talked about a parcel of helpless dandies, all
second, third, fourth, or fifth hand. That is to say, they
were not posing their own identities but were content to
trim themselves to patterns taken mechanically from
other people.

That concept of dandyism is central, I think, for an

understanding of what Whitman meant by the core of
reality in things—what Hopkins called the quiddity, the
hæcceitas or 'thisness'. He goes over and over again into
this question of first capturing your identity; before you
look out, be sure you know who is looking; let the looker
know himself, then what he looks at will be something
quite remarkable, it will be other people in a rather
special way, other people related in a quite new sort of
way to the experience of the individual looker. This helps
to solve a problem which has, in fact, been endemic in
modern literature, both British and American. The
problem arises when, under the impact of modern
psychology with its insistence on the dependence of
human consciousness on private trains of association, and
its view that all our consciousness is a continuous private
flow between retrospect and anticipation, the individual
comes to feel himself the prisoner of his unique consciousness, unable to make any gesture that can be properly
interpreted by others, unable, indeed, to communicate at
all. We insist more and more that every man is locked in
his private train of association, that the public gestures
that he gives, the flags he raises to signal to other people,
cannot ever really reflect what is going on in his essentially
private loneliness, and that the only way to communicate
and live in society at all is to empty the heart of its individuating vision. To use Elizabeth Bowen's phrase,
only by the "death of the heart" is social contact possible.
That is a tragic vision which runs through Miss Bowen's
work and also through Joyce's *Ulysses*, and in a different
way again through the novels of Lawrence, with their

exploration of the problem of the individual coming to terms with the core of otherness in other people.

How does Whitman's kind of rebellion solve this problem? He does it very interestingly. Instead of condemning man to lonely introspection, instead of condemning the stream of consciousness for ever to be moving privately, unanchored and lost and damned, as Septimus Warren Smith is in Virginia Woolf's novel *Mrs. Dalloway*, he explores ways of making the private stream of consciousness a means of assimilating the whole observed world to oneself, and setting up a new unity which consists of a special sort of relationship between the observer, the observed, and his environment—and not only his geographical environment. Those enormous catalogues of America at work, stratified now by geographical regions, now by historical moments, have for their function the bringing together of the perceiver and the perceived so that a new view of history, of time, of identity, of consciousness, of reality and, as Whitman would say, of the cosmos, is made possible.

Whitman was the great time-binder and space-binder. All the new techniques which he introduces into his poetry are devices for somehow solving the problem we all feel of life developing, slipping away into isolated fragments of time, isolated units of consciousness, which cannot make real contact with each other. He was a great rider of ferries and street-cars. One of his finest poems is 'Crossing Brooklyn Ferry', where he sees the ferry as the space-binder going to and fro connecting places, and the people going to and fro, changing their geographical

43

location. It is one of my favourite poems, because it discovers the perfect symbol of time, space, and diversity among people of geographical and chronological diversity. Whitman looks around and sees the sights and sounds of Brooklyn and of Manhattan, he sees the people, speculates on where they came from, what they are doing, their diverse occupations, interests, sufferings, thoughts, hopes, fears. One by one he enters into them, achieves a circumambient consciousness in which he and they are included, but always (and this is what is so impressive and original) starting from the clearly recognised individuated self.

In reading this poem and what Whitman has to say in his prose work about his obsession with ferries, I often think of an experience I had as a child and still have, and which must be very common. It is an experience which Robert Louis Stevenson describes most hauntingly in *A Child's Garden of Verses*. You are in a train and crossing a stretch of country and the train passes, say, a farm, and in front of the farm there is a man or a group of people working. You pass them, and you hate to pass them; you think: There he is, an individual living in a part of the country I am just being carried through; I want to stop, to see what sort of life it is. It is the same with the glimpses you get through windows of women washing dishes as you are carried by. I recall my impression of riding on the elevated railway in Chicago. Everyone leaves blinds open and you can look in and you have this extraordinary sense of being carried past individual lives, and you want to cry Stop! What does it mean to be a woman standing there washing dishes, a man sitting at a table? But you are carried relentlessly on and you have this curious elegiac feeling of loss.

It is precisely the fulfilment of this desire that Whitman achieves in his rather special kind of cataloguing techniques. He is not content to let them go. He carries them on with him poetically by the kind of consciousness with which he regards them. By surrendering to his own stream of consciousness he can recreate these people in their living objective reality. But the stream of consciousness must be carefully prepared and posed before you can do that.

There is one other point I want to emphasise, though of course I cannot talk about every aspect of Whitman. What is this elegiac note you get so brilliantly in 'Out of the Cradle Endlessly Rocking' and 'When Lilacs Last in the Dooryard Bloom'd'? There you have something which is the nearest Whitman ever gets to the Tennysonian or Victorian elegiac mode. Yet it is different in all sorts of ways—especially in its sense of time, of space, of other people. There is that extraordinary picture of Lincoln's coffin passing through the country and little groups of people watching it—for a moment you are projected into that group of people, and out again—and running right through are the great symbols of the lilac and the bird. It will not do just to quote a brief passage from either poem; these are tremendous cumulative developments that must be read at length to be properly appreciated. No poet is less good read in tiny snippets and it is unfair to Whitman to do that. There is a

dialectic working itself out in his best poems, particularly
'When Lilacs Last in the Dooryard Bloom'd'. 'Out of
the Cradle Endlessly Rocking' and 'When Lilacs Last in
the Dooryard Bloom'd' represent something remarkable,
a deliberate cultivating of a new kind of elegiac mood,
addressing oneself to death as part of the whole cosmic
process which includes life itself. This is very Whitmanesque and has led some of his more recent critics to
say he is really a gloomy death-wisher. But that I think
is radically to misunderstand Whitman's whole concept
of death as part of a cyclical, cosmic dance of life. Whitman sees this rhythm, this cosmic dance, everywhere—
even in a dung-heap. A dung-heap is refuse; it is also new
life. That concept of the rhythm of life is both elegiac
and hopeful. It is elegiac in the sense that we have to
prepare to lose ourselves in that sea, in that flux, in that
rhythm, but only ultimately to find ourselves in it. It is
the obverse of A. E. Housman's 'When you and I are
spilt on air Long we shall be strangers there'. It is much
more reminiscent of Mrs. Dalloway in Virginia Woolf's
novel when she wonders whether you can in death be
free at last of the tyrannising individuation of the self and
be spread among other people and really participate in
their lives.

In what respects, then, was Whitman a rebel, what did
he rebel against, and how fruitful was his rebellion? It
seems to me that his main objective was to come to terms
with the nature of identity, the nature of personality; to
explore new ways of relating a full relish of personal
identity with a full savouring of life existing in the teem-

ing world around him, whether of other people or of nature. What he rebelled against was the implication of the Victorian assumption that the poet must surrender either to elegy or to didacticism, the assumption that these are incompatible alternatives and, further, that directing of sensibility into pre-determined channels was the only way of writing a poem. What he won for the future in this rebellion was a new way of relating loneliness to love, the great perennial problem of modern literature. It was a way that involved a consciousness of the *otherness* of other people, a new kind of dependence on the conscious-ness closely akin to the stream-of-consciousness method in modern fiction, and a mode of poetical utterance which depended for its structure on a mosaic of ideas and impressions rather than on set forms.

And where does that take us? Precisely to the heart of the one great modern poet who has ignored and under-valued Whitman—Mr. Eliot himself. Whitman's Brook-lyn is not unlike Eliot's London. Both poets were similarly aware of the rhythms of modern life. Both used the mosaic of ideas, the special kind of poetic dialectic achieved by patterning fragments of the civilisa-tion you are presenting into a kind of eloquent and symbolic jigsaw. Whitman did that in his own way before Eliot did and it seems to me that no American poet, whether he accepts or rejects Whitman, can fail to have profited. It sometimes seems to me that the tragedy of Whitman is exactly the same as the tragedy of my native Scottish poet, Robert Burns. Both were admired for the wrong reasons and the people who imitated them most directly were the worst poets. The so-called Whitmanians of the twentieth century were those who cultivated a shrill patriotic rhetoric, but that is not the true Whitman idiom. I myself believe that the mosaic of ideas in Eliot, the stream of consciousness in the modern novel, and all those extraordinarily subtle devices through which the modern novelist and poet have tried to explore ways in which an individual sensibility can be modulated into an inclusive consciousness, are in the tradition of Whitman. How to escape the prison of the self and cultivate simultaneously self-consciousness and sympathy, using the sense of self-identity as a means of projecting oneself into the identity of others—that, I think, is Whitman's most valuable legacy to modern literature.

SINCLAIR LEWIS: A LOST ROMANTIC

BY GEOFFREY MOORE

THERE CAN HAVE BEEN FEW AMERICAN AUTHORS SO famous as Sinclair Lewis. He wrote twenty-two novels; he contributed two new terms to the mythology of the Western world; and he won the Nobel Prize. He was, in fact, an important man. Yet as a novelist—and I choose, perhaps a little unfairly, to understand by the term a writer who is concerned to explore through the medium of the novel the profoundest possibilities of the human spirit—as a novelist in this sense, he was second rate. In two novels, surely—that is, in *Main Street* and *Babbitt*—and in three others, possibly—that is, in *Arrowsmith*, *Elmer Gantry*, and *Dodsworth*—he raised himself, by an exercise of the imagination, above the level of sensibility of the *Saturday Evening Post*, for which he wrote in his early days; but so far as the remaining seventeen are concerned it seems to me that one would wish to preserve only a few speeches and a few character studies. Lewis is therefore by way of being a phenomenon and the question that his career raises is how one can be such a limited writer and also have such an important place in the history of Western literature.

What, I think, happened is this. Lewis was of a journalistic cast of mind, but he had rather more potentiality than is indicated by his early work, the pre-twenties novels and serials. He was an ideas man with ideals. He saw what could be done; he saw that the ordinary domestic American, the transatlantic equivalent of the Wells or Bennett character, had yet to be written about, and he did write about him—brightly, energetically, and with an amateurish conviction.

Europeans greeted Lewis with cries of joy when the novels of the 'twenties—*Main Street, Babbitt, Arrowsmith,* and *Elmer Gantry*—came out. Many Americans, on the other hand, were inclined to throw themselves on him with cries of rage. Did he not attack American institutions? "There was one good pastor in California," said Lewis, "who, upon reading my *Elmer Gantry*, desired to lead a mob and lynch me, while another holy man in the State of Maine wondered if there was no respectable and righteous way of putting me in jail." Other Americans seemed to regard him as an out-and-out humorist; the very idea that there could be any truth in his literary stunts was unthinkable. There is always a place in our minds to which we can consign the sort of disturbing thoughts that Lewis's novels arouse.

The approbation of Europe was the more remarkable because it came not only from ordinary readers but from European literary critics, and because it was capped by that Victoria Cross or Congressional Medal of Honour of literature, the Nobel Prize. This shows just how much we were in the dark, in the 'twenties, about what to expect from modern American literature. Hugh Walpole, in his Introduction to the English edition of *Babbitt*, said: "*Main Street*, the book with which Mr. Lewis won fame in the United States, seemed to many English readers an ugly book, dealing with ugly people. . . . At first sight it might seem as though Babbitt is guilty of the same crime. Let us admit at once that the English reader will find the first fifty pages difficult, the dialogue strange, the American business atmosphere obscure and complicated." We have moved a long way from the days when Walpole could say that, as has been shown by the award of the Nobel Prize to Hemingway and to Faulkner, novelists of quite different calibre. But it took twenty more years of increasing familiarity, and another world war, to make Europeans aware of American standards. In fact, in the 1920s Americans themselves were only just beginning to believe that they might have a literature worthy to rank with the other literatures of the world. The re-valuation of Melville was just beginning; Mark Twain was still a rather vulgar little humorist turned cynic who tried to settle down and write books that would come up to the standards of Nook Farm; Hemingway was that good-looking boxer and tennis player who worked for William Randolph Hearst in Paris; Faulkner was a boiler-room attendant in the University of Mississippi; the Fitzgerald of *This Side of Paradise* could hardly be taken seriously; and the decade of Steinbeck, Dos Passos, Wolfe, Caldwell, and Farrell had yet to come. Today, when the honourable roll of American novelists is called, the "Present" of Lewis sounds a little shrill beside the response of Hawthorne, Melville, Twain, James, Howells, Stephen Crane, Edith Wharton, Faulkner, and Hemingway. It is not merely a matter of inferior literary stature, obvious though that may be; it is a matter of emphasis too, and to understand why Lewis's limited point of view was so popular in the 'twenties we might briefly consider the social and intellectual climate of the second and third decades of the twentieth century in America.

For a decade before the First World War it seemed that something was happening in American literature. The first cuckoos had been heard long before 1912, the year of the 'poetic renaissance' in Chicago, when Harriet Monroe was publishing Sandburg, Lindsay and Masters, Eliot and Wallace Stevens. True, the sweet singers, Richard Hovey and Bliss Carman, were still singing their vagabond and fanciful songs, but these were also the years of Mabel Dodge's salon on Fifth Avenue, of Gertrude Stein's *Three Lives*, and of the discovery of Freud. Eugene O'Neill was writing those early plays that he carried in the famous suitcase to the Province Town Playhouse. Edna Millay was writing her first lyrics: 'Renaissance', that bone of contention, was published in *The Lyric Year* in 1912, and it is a good indication of the flame which possessed the rather soul-conscious literary aspirants of the time:

> "The soul can split the sky in two
> And let the face of God shine through,
> But East and West will pinch the heart
> That cannot keep them pushed apart;
> And he whose soul is flat—the sky
> Will cave in on him by and by."

These, too, were years of experiment with social ideas. In addition to *The Masses* and *New Republic* in New York, there was *Reedy's Mirror* in St. Louis, the magazine that published the first of Masters's poems, and Margaret Anderson's *Little Review* which turned like a weathervane to expound whatever creed or style might be fashionable at the moment. Lewis did not like the *Little Review*. "He hated," Grace Hegger Lewis recalls, "those arty, sophomoric little magazines." Yet, after all, the *Little Review* did publish, in addition to the silly people, Joyce, Yeats, Pound, and Gertrude Stein. This was, as Van Wyck Brooks put it, the time of America's "coming of age".

Then, after the war, that Cook's tour for some, that tomb for others, things were very different. The promise seemed to have gone, but the need for revolt was still there, and it was there in a harsher form; the mood was nihilistic. It was a transatlantic version of Dadaism, or the English 'Owenism' and the rather grotesque fancies of the Sitwells. The younger writers flaunted their disillusion like an honourable wound. Fitzgerald flirted with his in *This Side of Paradise*, Hemingway hinted at his in *In Our Time*, and Faulkner agonised over his in *Soldiers' Pay*. This sense of disillusion seemed to some Europeans a little exaggerated, even histrionic, because of the minor degree to which America had suffered in the First World War, but it was, I think, a measure of America's idealism. This 'lost' generation was in a sense also the 'found' generation. What they found was a common spirit of criticism. They left for Paris or Rome, or, if they did not leave their country, spent their time attacking American habits and institutions. Of these detractors perhaps the most important is Mencken, the scourger of the 'booboisie'.

Who were the 'boobs'? They were the dull and hypo-
critical members of American society, not just Middle
Westerners, although it is true that Mencken had little
liking for and less understanding of the workings of the
American mind beyond the Alleghenies. In the *Mercury*
he did what the *New Yorker* does in a much milder way
today, that is, pillory examples of muddled thinking and
general crassness. Here, for example, is an extract,
quoted by Mencken, from an ordinance passed by the
Christian Legislators of Long Beach, California: "No
person shall indulge in caresses, hugging, fondling, embracing, spooning, kissing, or wrestling with any person
or persons of the opposite sex . . . and no person shall sit
or lie with his or her head, or any other portion of his or
her person, upon any portion of a person or persons upon
or near any of the said public places in the city of Long
Beach." In lampooning such attitudes Mencken was
attacking what the young intellectuals of the time liked
to call 'puritanism'. Apart from sexual connotations,
puritanism signified practically anything one wished, like
not enjoying Gertrude Stein, or never having heard the
horn of Roland.

What was Lewis's attitude to all this? He was
attracted to some of Mencken's ideas, though he seemed
a little uneasy in this company. His ambivalent attitude may have had something to do with the matter
of 'art'. Mencken, like Edna Millay and the other
daring young things of the literary-bohemian set, regarded life as one thing and art as very much another.
This point of view nearly always results in pretty-

prettiness and attitudinising, and the bluff Middle Westerner in Lewis disliked it intensely—as his outburst against the *Little Review* showed. Yet all the time he had this very strain in him, as his early poems and stories reveal very clearly. He made the world triumph over Istra in *Our Mr. Wrenn*, but he allowed Fran Dodsworth and Carol Kennicott, who are much more sickeningly precious than Istra, to have their say. True, the world is made to triumph over them, too, in the end; but one feels that this was Lewis's reluctant following of the facts, rather than the result of a clear perception of exactly why and how Fran and Carol were wrong. To complicate matters, Lewis had firm convictions (although no very clear ideas) about his own artistic achievement. As the result of a review by Carl Van Doren in *The Nation* in 1921 he wrote furiously to Alfred Harcourt, protesting against Van Doren's "two assumptions":

"(1) that I am merely a disciple of Edgar Lee Masters in writing *M. St.*—somewhat humorous in that I have never sat down and read *Spoon River Anthology*, but merely heard parts of it read aloud, and this not until 1917, whereas I first began to plan *Main St.* 1905; and (2) that I have always been a writer of 'bright amusing chatter to be read at a brisk pace'. I asked him if he had read *The Job* or *Our Mr. Wrenn* or *Trail of the Hawk*, or certain short stories which I enumerated; and I hinted, if I did not say directly, that if he hadn't read these he had one devil of a nerve, and he was one devil of a bad critic, to dare to sum me up thus . . . You or Spingarn might follow this up by sending him a copy of *The Job* and making him read it. . . . I think he ought to do an entirely new article about me in *The Nation* . . . certainly he must change this if he's going to publish these articles in book form."

In another letter to Harcourt ten years later and just a month after the award of the Nobel Prize we find him comparing "Heywood Broun's supercilious words" in the *New York Times* with "Arnold Zweig's brilliant essay . . . spoken on the radio in Berlin and then published in the German *Literatur*; the comment of *l'Europe Nouvelle* in France; essays in *Das Tagebuch* in Germany; Dr. Karfeldt's analysis of my work before the huge and distinguished crowd at the formal prize-giving, with all the royalty there. . . ."

In order to understand the frame of mind which led Lewis to make these comments we must, I think, go back a little way and consider what kind of man he was. He was born in 1885 in a village rather like the Gopher Prairie of *Main Street*, a place called Sauk Centre in Minnesota. His father began as a schoolteacher but saved up enough money to take a two-year medical course in Chicago. He practised in Wisconsin, then moved to Minnesota. Three sons were born before his wife died of tuberculosis—Fred, Claud, and Harry Sinclair. Harry was five at the time his mother died and two years later his father married again. The population of Sauk Centre was 2,500, the people mostly German and Scandinavian in origin. Harry could never play as well as his brothers, and Grace Hegger Lewis in *Love from Gracie* seems to think that the effect on him of his brothers' derisive "Go chase yourself" was noticeable in later life. He retired

into a world of his own. He read *Robin Hood* and *Ivanhoe*.
In his freshman year at Yale, in 1904, he wrote a story of
which the title, 'A Miracle Forsooth', is sufficiently des-
criptive to need no further comment. At twenty-eight
years of age he was still writing 'Tennyson-and-water'
poems like this one, which begins:

> "Princess, princess, silver maiden,
> Throw your casement open; see—
> On the terrace I am singing,
> Come and take the road with me."

William Lyon Phelps says in his *Autobiography with
Letters* that Lewis was not disliked in college but "was
regarded with amiable tolerance, as a freak . . . He was a
complete and consistent individualist, going his own way,
and talking only about things which interested him. . . ."
He took some time off from Yale to join (as janitor)
Upton Sinclair's co-operative socialist colony, Helicon
Hall. Then he went off with a classmate; took a cattle-
boat to England, a journey which gave him the subject of
Our Mr. Wrenn; went back to Yale; graduated; got
various jobs on newspapers and in publishing firms; and
finally settled down in New York, where he married
Grace Hegger. It was while working as a publisher's
editor and commuting daily from Long Island that he
wrote his first five novels, during which time he gained
sufficient confidence to become a freelance.

Yet he was still a 'faery child', a fact which seems to be
of some importance in considering the nature of his satire.

He was a piner for mysterious places, for courts of love with royal jesters. He wrote a prayer to Grace Hegger at the time, which begins: "Our Father, Thou who hast made the faces of little children glad, and the field to shine with wonder upon Christmas Day—Thou who art so great that of Thee and thy ways the Jester can have but tiny glimmerings at the sunset time, or in beholding the goodness of the Lady Grace . . ." In his books Lewis tended to set his women on a pedestal, as Milt Daggett does with Claire in *Free Air* and as Dr. Kennicott does with Carol in *Main Street*. The other side of this romantic idealisation was a taste for lechery and his wife records that the first draft of *Elmer Gantry* was marred by his relish of this facet of Gantry's character. But, then, Mrs. Lewis may herself have aggravated this dichotomy in Lewis's personality. She seems, by her own account, to have contributed something, at least, to Lewis's persistent portraits of the blonde Lady Fair who says: "Don't you think it's a little icky, this sudden passion for embracing me when you're—well, exhilarated?"

After *Our Mr. Wrenn* Lewis turned to novels which can, by and large, be called 'romances'. Then he achieved fame, with *Main Street*, and he was never the same after that. Someone like Ludwig Lewisohn had only to say, "Mr. Lewis can contribute a great deal to American literature" and he would drop his current *Saturday Evening Post* serial and furiously start writing some book that would change the face of American literature. As he went on, he became more and more restless. He commuted, not from Long Island to New

York, but back and forth across the Atlantic. Finally, after the European accolade, this country boy who had made good (Lewis's style, attitude of mind, and public pronouncements invite the description) had earls to pick him up in their Rolls-Royces, and Bernard Shaw to ride up all pink and bearded on his bicycle to take tea with him. The Lewis story was, superficially, a success story, but as time went on the novels got worse and worse.

There is one pen portrait of him in the 'thirties that is very vivid—although of course romantically exaggerated —and that is the one by Thomas Wolfe in *You Can't Go Home Again*, where he writes of Sinclair Lewis as Lloyd McHarg, and says: "He was fantastically ugly, and to this ugliness was added a devastation of which George [George Webber, who is Wolfe] had never seen the equal." [In fact Lewis had developed skin cancer early in his married life and it was radium treatment which pockmarked his face and made it seem, as his wife said, 'spilt'.] "The first and most violent impression was his astonishing redness. Everything about him was red— hair, large protuberant ears, eyebrows, eyelids, even his bony, freckled, knuckly hands. . . . Moreover, it was a most alarming redness. His face was so red that it seemed to throw off heat, and if at that moment smoke had begun to issue from his nostrils and he had burst out in flames all over, George would hardly have been surprised. . . .

"He came towards George quickly, with his bony, knuckled hand extended in greeting, his lips twitching and bared nervously over his large teeth, his face turned

61

wryly upwards and to one side in an expression that was at once truculent, nervously apprehensive, and yet movingly eloquent of something fiercely and permanently wounded, something dreadfully lacerated, something so tender and unarmed in the soul and spirit of the man that life had got in on him at a thousand points and slashed him to ribbons. He took George's hand and shook it vigorously, at the same time bristling up to him with his wry and puckered face like a small boy to another before the fight begins, as if to say: 'Go on, now, go on. Knock that chip off my shoulder. I dare and double-dare you.' This was precisely his manner now, except that he said:

" 'Why you—why you monkeyfied—why you monkeyfied bastard, you! Just look at him!' he cried suddenly in a high-pitched voice, half-turning to his companions. 'Why you—who the hell ever told you you could write, anyway?' Then cordially: 'George, how are you? Come on in, come on over here!' "

I mentioned three stages in Lewis's work. One of them seems to me to extend from *Our Mr. Wrenn* (1914) to *Free Air* (1919)—the stage of the young Harry; another from *Main Street* (1920) to *The Man who Knew Coolidge* (1928)—the middle-aged Harry; and the third, the old Harry, from *Dodsworth* (1929) to *World So Wide* (1951). This is a tentative categorisation based on the areas of social life to which he devoted himself. One could make another set of categories depending on whether Lewis treated his characters from a rounded point of view, or satirically. In the first period the two novels that seem

to me most important are *Our Mr. Wrenn* and *Free Air*.
There is one peculiarly Lewis-like touch that is worth
quoting from *Our Mr. Wrenn*, that tale of the rabbit-like
man who took a cattle-boat across the Atlantic and, in
another land, learned a little about life. Wrenn meets a
Mr. Mittiford, Ph.D., in England, an American acad-
emic, and he says about him: "He wrote poetry which he
filed away under the letter 'P' in his poetry file." Wrenn
fights with the tough men on the ship, he meets a
socialist called Harry Morton, and he meets Istra Nash,
one of those icy-cold and yet attractive blonde bohemian
types that turn up so frequently in Lewis's novels. Istra
and he go for a 'daring' walk at night through the
English countryside to an equally daring colony. The
'message' of this book is really the same as the 'message'
of all those early novels, and that is that the dull people
are really the nicest people. At least they are honest. If
you stray into the world of Bohemia, of 'artiness', then
you will come to phoniness and to grief. Wrenn is
misled by his Istra but he settles down with the nice
people, the man who sells tobacco round the corner, the
people who tell crude jokes but who are really good at
heart.

The Job of 1917 has a woman as heroine. It is a 'fore-
runner' of *Main Street*. Una Golden is an office worker
with the soul of a blue-stocking. She revolts from the
village (in Pennsylvania), and the novel is really devoted
to trying to give you some feeling about the mystic
function of business. One can see Lewis 'trying out'
various themes, the theme of revolt, for example, and of

whether business is a suitable subject for a writing man with pretensions to 'art'.

When we come to Milt Daggett's story in *Free Air*— or Claire Boltwood's story; it could be called either—we have a number of indications of the central split in Lewis, the degree to which he wished to express his appreciation of the prairie people, and the degree, also, to which he felt abashed before the sophisticated, educated Easterners. There is one passage in which he seems to be describing himself: "Who is this extraordinary Milt Daggett? Him? Oh, nobody 'specially. He's just a fellow down here at Schoenstrom. But we all know him. Goes to all the dances, thirty miles round. The thing about him is: if he sees something wrong, he picks out some poor fellow like me and says what he thinks." And in another passage: "With Mr. Jones (that is, James Martin Jones, B.A.) he discussed—no, ye Claires of Brooklyn Heights, this garage-man and this threadbare young superintendent of a paint-bare school, talking in a tongue that was only a comma on the line, did not discuss corn-growing, nor did they reckon to guess that by heck the constabule was carryin' on with Widdy Perkins. They spoke of fish-culture, Elihu Root, the spiritualistic evidences of immortality, government ownership, self-starters for flivvers and the stories of Irvin Cobb."

Through Claire Boltwood we find out a great deal about Lewis's Middle West, but we find out more later through Carol Kennicott. I consider *Main Street* the best book Lewis ever wrote, partly for this reason and partly because in it he achieved a compromise between the two viewpoints I have mentioned, which were also the two sides of his nature. These two sides of Sinclair Lewis are represented by Carol, who is the person who wants to bring culture to Gopher Prairie and yet is rather snobbish, superior, and fanciful; and Dr. Kennicott, who is homely and good-natured, dedicated and dull. The book leaps like an electric spark between the poles of Carol's disgust and Main Street's healthy philistinism.

With *Babbitt*, satire begins. It was the attempt that Lewis made to prove himself as an artist. The characters are more obviously caricatures, and the prose has the bite of winter air in Minnesota. The raw material of the novel is forced into a light-hearted pattern by the satiric intention. Lewis is not here 'opening himself' to life; he is deciding what should be said and forcing his characters into this mould. It is a fantasy, really, on the theme of business, an attack on the hypocrisy of small business-men, but with a certain undertone of friendliness.

In *Arrowsmith* we have a rather fuller picture despite a similar satirical intention. The heart of the book is a rather unsmiling portrait of the scientist, Lewis's great hero, Max Gottlieb. Otherwise, it is an indictment of how business can use research unscrupulously for its own end, and it side-swipes the great foundations. It might be said to be the story of Mr. Truthseeker.

Elmer Gantry is, by contrast, a novel about Mr. Opportunist. It satirises the misuse of religion and contains the unforgettable portrait of Frank Shallard, who is beaten up by religious people for speaking on behalf of free-thinking. Gantry falls in with Sharon Faulkner, the evangelist.

The book is a study of hypocrisy; and I find myself going back, while reading it, to what Lawrence said in *Studies in Classical American Literature* about Hawthorne—how everything is fine on the surface while that blue-eyed *wunderkind* of a Nathaniel keeps up the pretence, but how underneath there are things going on, disagreeable things. This is of course not an unknown phenomenon outside the United States, but although the matter of puritanism is sometimes exaggerated, it does seem as if the Calvinistic strain in American culture might have made the discrepancy between public and private morality more acute than elsewhere. There are two rebels in *Elmer Gantry*—Shallard and Zecklin. Zecklin, who is a man of the Max Gottlieb type, is against conformity. There is no underlying praise of the Middle Western ethos as there had been in *Main Street*. The life seems to have gone from these Middle Western people; they have sold out and gone to California.

The Man who Knew Coolidge (1928) is a satire in dialogue. Babbitt has become rotten. This boom-man is cliché-ridden and disgusting. Babbitt did have good qualities; he was lovable as well as despicable. Lowell Schmaltz, however, has no good qualities, no aspirations, no brain—nothing but grossness. He represents the depths of Lewis's disgust, and Lewis tried to redeem the picture to some extent in his next novel, which, socially speaking, goes into what I have tentatively called the final period. *Dodsworth* is about an upper-class Babbitt with his good points left in, rather than sieved out to serve the purpose of satire. Sam Dodsworth is a motor

manufacturer who cares intensely for what he is doing.
He is a craftsman, almost an artist, but temperamentally
he is incompatible with his wife, Fran, who is the daughter
of a brewer and has cultural pretensions. In her one sees
the familiar divorce of life and ideals. Her ideals do not
arise out of the pattern of her life; they come from another
culture entirely. It is European pretentiousness that she
longs for and that she gets, disastrously, in the end. She
commits adultery, wants to run off with her Austrian
Count, and is only brought to her senses when the Count
brings his mother along to get him out of it. Mother
effectively prevents him marrying her; then she goes back
to Sam, and everything is fine for a time. But at the end
her selfishness drives him off. Sam is to blame a bit,
because he thinks too constantly of the world of business
and not enough of his wife. It is a picture of the American
boy-man, the 'mythical' archetype, the man who is
emotionally unawakened but is at heart an idealist.
Dodsworth is a novel that has a great deal in it, and one of
Lewis's more important ones.

In *Ann Vickers* Lewis deals with the life of an emancipated woman who has an illegitimate child, and learns
from her experience. He seems to be letting himself go in
this book. It is, in fact, as if he were beginning to find
out something about life and emotions. There is a rather
intense concentration on things of the flesh.

The last books are watered-down versions of what
Lewis had done before. Even *It Can't Happen Here*, which
is about the best of them, has an off-centre, fantastic
quality about it that makes one not able to believe in, to

feel for, the novel as a whole. There are moments of
wonderfully effective satire, as in the characterisation of
Bishop Prang, but the other attitudes and conversations
ring false; they are exaggerated beyond necessity, and the
opposition of Doremus Jessup, the good editor, and Buzz
Windrip, the dictator, somehow goes wrong.

Then, towards the last, we have the picture of
Frederick William Cornplow in *The Prodigal Parents*, a
Babbitt type: "Like most Americans he was profoundly
democratic except perhaps as regards social standing,
wealth, political power and club membership." But at
least this book deals with 'real' American life again. In
Bethel Merriday Lewis turns to the theatrical world; in
Gideon Planish, in 1943, to satire of 'do good' institutions.
Then we have the story of a judge in Minnesota (not the
mythical State of Winnemac; it is called Minnesota in
Cass Timberlane); *Kingsblood Royal* about the Negro
situation, *The God-Seeker*, and finally *World So Wide*, in
which a man kills his wife rather conveniently by
accident, and then goes off to get an education in Italy.

If one can say that Lewis has a 'typical' technique it is
the technique of his satirical novels, in which the approach
is theoretical and intellectual. He has more in common
with the popular English writers of the period than with
the American. He looked to H. G. Wells, to Galsworthy,
to Hugh Walpole, indicating the difference between the
American writer of the 'twenties and the American writer
of today. Lewis's method was to choose an institution or
a class of people, decide on a point of view, and then
flatten his characters into the mould he desired. It is a

sort of 'wide spectrum' writing; the awareness is a 'public' awareness; there is no 'innerness'. If you take the example of the alarm clock in *Babbitt*, he describes it from the point of view of its manufacture. When he treats emotional relationships he does so in rather the same sort of way, as, I suppose, a journalist would (I do not use the word journalist in a pejorative sense exactly, but rather to indicate the level of the discussion). There is evidence in his books, supported by what Grace Hegger says in *Love from Gracie*, that it was not until the 1930s that he began finding out what life was all about; and then it was too late. His style had been set, and he could not go back.

In a way Lewis was a rebel with too many causes. He was rebelling against the idea that Middle Westerners were inferior to sophisticated, cultured Easterners in the early books, and he was rebelling against hypocrisy of all kinds in the later ones. One aspect of his rebellion he wrote about himself. "*Main Street,*" he said, "published late in 1920 was my first novel to rouse the embattled peasantry and it had a success of scandal. One of the most treasured American myths was that all American villagers were particularly noble and happy and here an American attacked the myth. Scandalous! Some hundreds of thousands read the book with the same masochistic pleasure that one has in sucking an aching tooth."

When he began *Main Street* he called it *The Village Virus*. He wrote three drafts, beginning the first one as early as 1905 when still at Yale. The title is indicative.

He was against the smugness and complacency of the prairie villages—but with love, because he was part of that world; then he switched from that to a class, the small businessman; then, to the medical profession, to the religious 'profession', to 'do good' institutions, to the Negro question, and so on. There were unlimited topics for him to choose from and, restlessly, he went from one to the other. He woke people up by dramatising social evils.

Like Wells, after whom he named his son, he had in him as much of the reformer as the novelist. Yet like Wells, too, he had his felicities as a writer and I should not feel that I had done justice to his achievement if I left the impression that, in my opinion, he was entirely without literary merit.

In the first place one must admit thas he created a world of his own and peopled it with characters who make sense within its confines. It is a Dickensian type of talent. This is why I usually find myself objecting to the unqualified use of the term 'realistic' with which American literary historians so often label Lewis.

In a sense, yes, he is realistic, but not in the way in which this term is usually used in literary criticism. He is realistic in that he writes about ordinary people and ordinary happenings. In other words, I think that Mrs. Lewis is right when she says that "he was in a sense more typical of people in the twenties in America than Fitzgerald was". Alfred Kazin, reviewing *Main Street* in the *New York Times*, picked this out and was very hard on it, but he was looking at literature from the point of view of art, whereas Mrs. Lewis, no literary critic, was looking on the book from the point of view of the ordinary reader, in terms of life itself. In terms of life, *Main Street* and *Babbitt* were nearer to ordinary American existence than *This Side of Paradise* and *The Great Gatsby*. It is this sense of life that Lewis manages to project despite the grotesqueness, despite the cardboard nature, of his characterisation. One can say that he did succeed in conveying the reality of Middle Western people, even though one has the starker example of Dreiser before him. Moreover, he is not as bad as all that, as a prose writer. One has only to look at the first paragraph of *Babbitt* to see that at his best he could write a clean, stripped-down kind of prose that is fanciful but avoids excesses. "The towers of Zenith aspired above the morning mist; austere towers of steel and cement and limestone, sturdy as cliffs and delicate as silver rods. They were neither citadels nor churches, but frankly and beautifully office-buildings. The mist took pity on the fretted structures of earlier generations: the Post Office with its shingle-tortured mansard, the red-brick minarets of hulking old houses, factories with stingy and sooted windows, wooden tenements coloured like mud." It is not the prose of 'sensuous immediacy' but it is an emotive prose that has power to it and the attraction of lucidity as well as emotional undertones.

Did Lewis, as the Nobel Prize judges maintained, create new types and "high-class American humour"? His characters *seem* to be new types because they have strange manners, and they come from a strange place—

strange to Europeans at that time, that is—but it seems to me that they are really types that we know about in Europe too. And as for American humour, yes, in a way, and yet there is not the roughness and the gusto of Artemus Ward or Mark Twain. The humour is a little thin. It is neither the Ring Lardner or *New Yorker* dead-pan type of humour, nor the exaggerated humour of that older time; it falls unsuccessfully between the two. However, I must remember that I had set myself at this point—out of a sense of duty to the very real force of this remarkable man—to pick out his good qualities. He does, let us say, give us portraits of Americans that we can, despite the fantasy of the scenes, believe in and understand. They are old types who have been trans-formed by a new country.

If I may sum up, then: in his early days Lewis was a romantic, a Booth Tarkington with a star in his eye, and he did better than he knew, particularly in *Main Street*. This changed him, and he attempted 'art'. He achieved fame because the American public was in a mood to hear the things he said, and because the European public, rather in the dark and also a little anti-American, admired *Babbitt* for reasons which were not exactly literary. He gave Europeans the sort of America they wanted to read about.

When I re-read Lewis I am struck by two strong and conflicting impressions. The first impression is one of annoyance. I am annoyed by the shallowness of his writing, by his lists of places seen and things done, by his attempt to capsule whole areas of emotion and render them in a single paragraph of reportorial neighbourliness, by those caricature-characterisations that Alfred Kazin called his "brilliant equivalents" of American people. And yet, for all this initial feeling of annoyance, I come back always to a feeling of sympathy for these grotesque people he created. This second impression is one that leads me to the man himself—I think it is without any intention on Lewis's part or any conscious intention on mine—to this cantankerous soul who was driven by the everlasting gospel of work and whose good heart shines through his work. All these books of his reflect back on him, but since he did not consciously intend it, the result is somehow acceptable. I feel that I can agree with Thomas Wolfe when he goes on in that account of Lewis-McHarg in *You Can't Go Home Again*: "In spite of the brevity of their acquaintance, George had already seen clearly and unmistakably what a good and noble human being McHarg really was. He knew how much integrity and courage and honesty was contained in that tormented tenement of fury and lacerated hurts. Regardless of all that was jangled, snarled, and twisted in his life, regardless of all that had become bitter, harsh, and acrid, McHarg was obviously one of the truly good, the truly high, the truly great people of the world."

Max Gottlieb in *Arrowsmith*, the scientist, the kind of selfless, dedicated human being that Lewis admired, says: "God give me a quiet and relentless anger at pretence and all pretentious work and all work left slack and unfinished. God give me a restlessness whereby I may neither sleep nor accept praise till my observed results

F

equal my calculated results or in pious glee I discover and assault my error. God give me strength not to trust in God!" Lewis's relentless anger and his restlessness lasted all his life, though we might have our doubts about some of the targets that he used these qualities against. In the end he had nothing to write about except the same watered-down old topics.

I am half-inclined to say that America has outgrown Lewis. In the Gopher Prairies of the 'fifties the bankers have been to Williams or to Yale and even the store-keepers have a degree from the State university. But it is more than just a matter of education. If *Main Street*, *Babbitt*, *Arrowsmith*, *Elmer Gantry*, and *The Man who Knew Coolidge* capture anything of the spirit of their time, then the Middle West has changed a great deal in the past thirty years. Yet Lewis's characters were, after all, carica-tures even for that time. In his early books he praised 'small-town' qualities, and then he jumped on the band-wagon of the 'twenties and dramatically illustrated Mencken's prejudices. He might—and he did say this to a European audience—he might have loved the Babbitt of his youth, but Babbitt changed, and Lewis did not change with him. America, in other words, had proved herself bigger than Sinclair Lewis. He tried to tackle too many of the social and moral problems of America in his time and his attempts grew progressively more shallow and less successful. He was ambitious, hard-working, and idealistic, but he was not exceptionally intelligent or gifted; nor was he equipped with a sensibility or a power of understanding above the average. He could not feel greatly, and that was his limitation and also his strength. His picture is often distorted, therefore; the colours clash; the point of focus is wrong. He did a lot of harm, but he also did a lot of good, and, at the very least, one cannot help admiring the sheer effort of his attempt—or perhaps, more accurately, standing aghast at the feverish activity of this driven, impossibly lonely man. Mark Schorer tells us that when he had his last heart attack in Florence, the doctor who came to see him found that the decanter by his bed contained not water but straight Bourbon. I should not be surprised to learn that in the drawer of the bedside table there was a Gideon Bible. Lewis was a travelling man, and he had a lot in common with the drummers that he talks about in *Free Air*: ". . . not only were they the missionaries of business, supplementing the taking of orders by telling merchants how to build up trade, how to trim windows and treat customers like human beings, but also . . . they, as much as the local ministers and doctors and teachers and newspapermen, were the agents in spreading knowledge and justice. It was they who showed the young men how to have their hair cut—and to wash behind the ears and shave daily; they who encouraged villagers to rise from scandal and gossip to a perception of the Great World of politics and sports, and some measure of art and science." "These travelling men," Lewis says, "were pioneers in spats," and I think it is a sufficiently incongruous and a sufficiently true image to stand as Lewis's epitaph. He was himself, in a sense, a pioneer in spats.

If we say that America has changed, in the sense that it

has outgrown Lewis, his books will pass into history along with the flivvers and the Kittyhawks and the unfenced prairie. Yet even as I say this I can see the ghost of Lewis with his head cocked on one side saying: "Will they? Will they pass into history?" And this is the sort of healthy attitude one ought to be left with when one reaches any thumping conclusion. Has America outgrown Lewis? The banker, I said, goes to Yale and the storekeeper to the State university. A thousand increments of commercially or altruistically motivated lessons in culture, in learning, in sophistication, have transformed the social scene in America; yet hypocrisy, provincialism, prejudice, all forms of materialism, have only changed their clothes to mingle, as they have always done, with the crowd. New writers—Mary McCarthy, for example —are better equipped to describe these clothes. But the face—is it not the same face that Lewis saw? Perhaps also we ought to remember, when we use Lewis's novels in order to point sarcastically at America, that the attitudes of mind in *Main Street, Babbitt, Arrowsmith,* and *Elmer Gantry* are not peculiar to America. To point at America is also to point at ourselves.

SCOTT FITZGERALD:
BEDEVILLED PRINCE CHARMING

BY WALTER BEZANSON

IN 1920 IT WAS ALL THERE WAITING: EXHILARATION, hunger for excitement, an urge for new adventures. Let yourself go, baby! Come on, climb on board, this is it; the hell with what anybody says! The new idiom extended through speech, manners, belief—or was it unbelief? It brought new images, male and female. The college boy with his racoon coat and his hip flask rode by in an old jalopy or an open roadster. The flapper of John R. Held's cartoons and the cover-girls of *New Masses* revelled in strange side-swipe hats, tight short skirts, bobbed hair, silk stockings, shoes easy to kick off when the dancing really got going. These youngsters cherished five big outlets. Jazz: the hot music that had come upriver when Storyville in New Orleans was closed down; as war came on and fear for the city's morals grew, the skin-and-bones men took boats to Kansas City, Memphis, and Chicago; hot jazz was the new music for a new time. Liquor: forbidden by Prohibition, it became a necessity. Money: boom days these were; what you didn't have already you could buy. Sex: all free, and such fun. Talk: serious talk, cynical talk, rebellious talk, fast talk.

And so the show went on the road, boisterously. Up front in his precious white sweater, wearing his clean white flannels like a cheer-leader at the big game, came F. Scott Fitzgerald, late of Princeton and author, 1920, of *This Side of Paradise*; and of course walking beside him that lovely, lovely wild blonde Zelda, from Montgomery,

Alabama. The very pitch and tone of Fitzgerald's entry on the scene is in this first book of his: "Amory's suggestion was that they should each order a Bronx, mix a broken glass in it, and drink it off. To his relief no one applauded the idea, so having finished his high-ball, he balanced his chin in his hand and his elbow on the table—a most delicate, scarcely noticeable sleeping position, he assured himself—and went into a deep stupor. . . .

"He was awakened by a woman clinging to him, a pretty woman, with brown, disarranged hair and dark blue eyes.

" 'Take me home!' she cried.

" 'Hallo!' said Amory, blinking.

" 'I like you,' she announced tenderly.

" 'I like you too.'

"He noticed that there was a noisy man in the background and that one of his party was arguing with him.

" 'Fella I was with's a damn fool,' confided the blue-eyed woman. 'I hate him. I want to go home with you.'

" 'You drunk?' queried Amory with intense wisdom.

"She nodded coyly.

" 'Go home with him,' he advised gravely. 'He brought you.'

"At this point the noisy man in the background broke away from his detainers and approached.

" 'Say!' he said fiercely. 'I brought this girl out here and you're butting in!'

"Amory regarded him coldly, while the girl clung to him closer.

" 'You let go that girl!' cried the noisy man.

"Amory tried to make his eyes threatening.

" 'You go to hell!' he directed finally, and turned his attention to the girl.

" 'Love first sight,' he suggested.

" 'I love you,' she breathed and nestled close to him. She *did* have beautiful eyes.

"Someone leaned over and spoke in Amory's ear.

" 'That's just Margaret Diamond. She's drunk and this fellow here brought her. Better let her go.'

" 'Let him take care of her, then!' shouted Amory furiously. 'I'm no Y.W.C.A. worker, am I?—am I?'

" 'Let her go!'

" 'It's *her* hanging on, damn it! Let her hang!' "

Well, this is a boy writing, and writing rather well, of his first adventures on the new scene. He could also write badly: "Suddenly he felt an overwhelming desire to let himself go to the devil—not to go violently as a gentleman should, but to sink safely and sensuously out of sight. He pictured himself in an adobe house in Mexico, half-reclining on a rug-covered couch, his slender, artistic fingers closed on a cigarette while he listened to guitars strumming melancholy undertones to an age-old dirge of Castile and an olive-skinned, carmine-lipped girl caressed his hair. Here he might live a strange litany, delivered from right and wrong and from the hound of heaven and from every God (except the exotic Mexican one who was pretty slack himself and rather addicted to Oriental scents)—delivered from success and hope and poverty into that long chute of indulgence which led, after all, only to the artificial lake of death." Both passages are to be understood in terms of the mood summarised at the end of *This Side of Paradise*: "Here was a new generation, shouting the old cries, learning the old creeds, . . . grown up to find all Gods dead, all wars fought, all faiths in man shaken. . . ."

Now the social scene of the 'twenties ran deeper than either my opening remarks or Fitzgerald's first book would suggest. In 1920 the population of America, having almost doubled in a matter of three or four decades, was 105 million, and the country was becoming intensively urban. New York in its skyline proclaimed itself the flamboyant capital of the new era. Some 40 per cent of Americans were now living in urban areas (cities of more than 8,000), and while such concentrations were an old story in Europe they were new in the 3,000-mile east-west stretch of America. Moreover some 35 million immigrants had come into the States in the century 1820–1920, the movement reaching its height with over a million annually just before the war. What was different about this last influx was that the balance of the newest Americans were from southern and eastern Europe. The effects of this mass migration came to a head in the 'twenties and created problems. For many of the immigrants themselves the situation seemed often hopeless, though it was hope that had brought them there in the first place. Housing, transportation, city jobs, and the new institutions were baffling to peasant families trying to find old ways in a new world. For the Americans already there, predominantly English in stock, culture, and background, there were problems arising at once from the fact of these new immigrants—problems in religion, language, labour, social theory, and social welfare. Beneath the gay bravado of the 'twenties were serious social tensions.

Now and then an event in history gets blown up to undue size and takes on symbolic importance. One may ask why, about such an event. Typical of this period, then, was the Sacco-Vanzetti trial stretching across the decade from 1920 to 1927. I would hope that only young people here would have to be reminded what this famous case was about. Presumably guilty of murder when imprisoned in 1920, these two poor Italians were tried and re-tried in an arena cluttered with pleas, interventions, new hearings, and a special committee of review. Nicola Sacco and Bartolomeo Vanzetti died that summer of 1927 in the state prison in Massachusetts, and with them for some there died an aspect of American life. Writers, intellectuals, university people, and plain citizens had fought this thing from the beginning in the name of social justice; the two men—admitted radicals, anarchists, and draft-dodgers—maintained to the end that they were not murderers, and this of course was the issue. There is a phrase in the trial text that says the guilty men "ran like Italians", and another element for some was that, whether or not Sacco and Vanzetti had murdered, they were the kind of people who did such things. In the nice town where I then lived as a boy, three miles from the New England court-house where they were convicted, the general sentiment I recall was that "they got what was coming to them". So that I feel, as many others have in the past, the shame of such an event, but also pride that it became an event and was not simply something done in a dark corner, and that it brought people to their feet.

Fitzgerald was not one who could stand up to such a cause. This was not his kind of world, a fact which sets one kind of limit as we look back at him, trying to judge the sort of 'young rebel' he may have been.

In the realm of politics, serenely presiding over such problems, were two of the least qualified and one of the most unlucky Presidents. The primary asset of Harding, the Ohio front-man, was summed up in what a lady I knew said: "But he so *looks* like a President!" At Harding's death, sworn in by candlelight in a Vermont farmhouse, came Cal Coolidge, that tight-lipped folk figure of the back country who believed in virtue and rocking-chairs and keeping his mouth shut. The unlucky one was Herbert Hoover, a wealthy and able mining engineer whose humane instincts and general initiative were firmly fastened to nineteenth-century concepts of the conduct of government. There were significant figures on the margin of national politics—men like the vigorous Bob La Follette of Wisconsin and the burly Irish-Catholic Governor of New York, Al Smith, but both missed the Presidency. In retrospect the 'twenties were a political vacuum between the idealism and reform achievements of the Wilson era and the bold pragmatism of Franklin Roosevelt's New Deal of the 'thirties. "The business of the United States Government," said farmer Coolidge, "is business," and so it became. It was the era of real estate booms, the big money, the fast dollar; a time when house servants listened at the pantry door to overhear investment tips from the dinner guests; when Henry Ford was putting an unbroken line of Model T's on the road and paying his workers the unheard-of wage of five dollars a day. Prosperity and technology combined to give the luckier young people a sense that the sky was the limit. Fitzgerald at first was one of them.

The 'twenties spawned a youth cult. Wars are fought by young men and I suppose it is fair and inevitable that they and their girls should come to power when war is over. What the new power was used against can be estimated by a glance into some children's books of the past—treasuries, as they are, of past manners and morals. We note the tiny, colonial *New England Primer*, massive with dogmas relegating any slim chance of joy to the after-world; the Rollo books of mid-nineteenth century, with their prim emphasis on right behaviour; and the Alger books of the late nineteenth century, telling children how to be successful in the market place through frugality and early rising. Jumping suddenly to a post-Fitzgerald cartoon of the *New Yorker*, we see the guests at a fashionable dinner party confronted with an impudent little face peering through the *portière*: "Everybody in this room but me is a son-of-a-bitch!" Though it is certain enough that the Kingdom of Brat did not really take over middle-class American life, it was there to be reckoned with. A new generation was dancing round the old, and Scott Fitzgerald was one of the people calling the tune and even composing it. He was not really up to a diabolic role, however, and the paradox is that, seen from this distance, the image looks quite otherwise: a charming, almost virginal, golden-haired young man with green eyes storming the outer walls of the Wicked City.

Fitzgerald's life exhibits both phases of that mobility, geographical and social, so characteristic of American life. It began with his flight, from a provincial Irish family on the upper reaches of the Mississippi, to the upper-class world of the Princeton campus. After going south to an army training camp he whirled on through high life in New York, Paris, and the Riviera, and then came 'home'; but he was to shuttle back and forth until the end. His restless quest for movement and glamour ended fittingly, if tragically, in Hollywood. He both cherished and fought his rootlessness, as have many American writers before him and after. In the 'twenties it was being said that when Mark Twain came east he may have hurt himself, becoming over-civil and surrendering to gentility. Fitzgerald was among the young mid-western writers who went still farther east until they came to Paris; when he went home, it was not to settle down in, or even write about, Minnesota. He was, I think, geographically rootless as well as heart-breakingly anxious to be at the top. His personal equipment included a consuming ambition to be someone, an Irish flair for erratic but warm personal display, and an instinct for being at the centre of the limited social world that stirred him—the clubs and campuses of the Ivy League, estate life in Long Island or Maryland, the luxury hotels of New York, Paris, the Mediterranean, or wherever else he could luxuriate and see lovely girls; his passion for beauty included the sheer scenery of wealth.

As he continued to circle wider and faster it became clear that his deeper alienation was psychic. The characteristic episodes of his career show extraordinary instability in everything relating to money and alcohol. Zelda's losing fight with schizophrenia was matched by his own deepening fears for her and himself. Fitzgerald's efforts to grapple with these things—honest but theatrical —are recorded in his pieces which Edmund Wilson gathered for *The Crack-Up*. At the centre there was a *malaise*, real disharmony. He was not the first artist to experience that, of course. His psychology seems curiously like that of Edgar Allan Poe in some ways. Poe endured even more savage torments over money and alcohol, and his restless moves among the cities of the American east—Boston, Providence, New York, Philadelphia, Baltimore, Charleston—parallel Fitzgerald's international sallies. Both tended to write fragmentarily and for periodicals, and between achievements both spiralled up and then down, way down. Scott Fitzgerald, with his outward reputation as chronicler of the 'twenties, a kind of laureate of the jazz age, the man who wrote, as Gertrude Stein said, the bible of flaming youth, was a driven human being.

In spite of fundamental tensions and temperamental excesses, which perhaps the artist not only may have but must have, Fitzgerald somehow managed six novels, of which four are of consequence. *This Side of Paradise*, though no longer artistically satisfying, is still amusing and interesting. Three others—*The Great Gatsby* (1925), *Tender is the Night* (1934), and the unfinished *The Last Tycoon* (1941)—are all very much to be reckoned with. The short stories, four collections plus other stories in magazines or unpublished, add to a total of some 160; they run an astonishing gamut from trash to art. The novels, the stories, and the miscellany of *The Crack-Up* (1945), then, are what he was capable of in spite of everything. Even his early death in 1940 did not bring a renascence of his lost reputation. A dominant figure of the 'twenties, Fitzgerald's name had faded fast in the 'thirties. Not having the head or heart for either Marxism or anti-Marxism in that decade, he was lost among the social-documentary group of the day. It was from an isolated position that he published *Tender is the Night* in the mid-thirties. Then, almost before he knew it, his time was up, and from a bed in California he was trying desperately to finish *The Last Tycoon*, which really promised to be good. He was gone, and not much missed. After the Second World War *The Crack-Up* brought him back, and I should guess that this was partly because after one war people became interested in what it had been like after another, but even more, in America at least, because this almost religiously documentary account of the turmoil of Fitzgerald's existence spoke directly to a new generation of young people for whom Freud was not just fashionable but a primary value. The word got round that Fitzgerald had great sensitivity to his own bedevilment, and it became clear, with the publication of Arthur Mizener's good biography in 1951, that there had been more to him than a raw sensitivity to personal experience and a need to try to get it all down. If he had that romantic intensity which so captivated his compatriots, he also was capable at times of standing apart and looking at himself and his material, of keeping his æsthetic distance.

Gatsby is certainly Fitzgerald's best work, and as such may also serve as touchstone for the question of his rebellion. It is the story of Nick Carraway, the narrator, and what he made out of Jay Gatsby, nominal hero of the book. Gatsby had changed his name from James Gatz at the age of seventeen because of a dream; Carraway's job is to uncover that dream. The story is closely plotted, firmly developed, tightly considered. Its action occurs wholly in the summer of 1922, and as the story opens Nick has just taken a small house on Long Island next door to the great mansion of the mysterious, wealthy, much-rumoured-about Gatsby. The leaves are green, it is June, the air is soft. At the end of the story, after the principal characters have criss-crossed and been involved and embittered and hurt, Gatsby lies murdered in the swimming-pool beside his mansion (a scene dramatically recovered, you will remember, in the movie *Sunset Boulevard*). Now the leaves are falling, and a little cluster of them float by the mattress on which lies the body of Gatsby as it slowly turns in the blue water.

Who was this man Gatsby? What did he mean? What did he stand for? Involved in mysterious affairs which were probably corrupt, he yet stirred Nick's imagination. Gatsby's single joy was his lavish, flamboyant parties. There on the open lawns by the sea, where the hanging lanterns reflected in Long Island Sound, people came and went, came and went; nobody particularly invited, everybody particularly invited. And there stood Gatsby himself, not drinking, faultlessly attired in the bad taste of a pink suit. Doing what? Why? Gatsby called Nick "old sport", took him to New York city to meet Wolfsheim, the man who fixed the World Series in 1919. But who *was* Gatsby? Some said he ran a chain of drugstores; some said he was related to the Kaiser; some said he was a bootlegger; some said he had killed a man (they generally said this when they saw him in certain moods). Nick cannot keep from devoting his summer to trying to make him out.

The kind of young man Nick is conditions his answer. He is called early, in jest, "the rose"—a young innocent. He wears white flannels. He decently tends his business at the Probity Trust in New York. "I am slow thinking and full of interior rules," he says, and, "I am one of the few honest people I have ever known." Thus as he gradually learns of Gatsby's past—that he *is* a bootlegger and has made big money the fast way—one might expect that the probity-conscious young man from Minnesota would see only another instance of the corruption which he has everywhere found. He has already been repelled by the almost obscene hardness of Tom Buchanan, old friend of days at Yale, who lives across the bay with his lovely wife Daisy. One by one the people in the story are shown in their venality. But Gatsby, the outwardly corrupt one and the man with no background, proves a man of interior dimensions. Gatsby, Nick learns, is a man possessed by a dream. The dream is a girl, Daisy Buchanan. Gatsby and Daisy had been in love years ago, but while at the war he had lost her to the rich and pre-possessing Buchanan. Now that Gatsby has made his money—and he made it to be near Daisy and perhaps win her back—he gives his parties, lighting up his big house night after night and watching for Daisy among the people who come and go. And night after night, when the party is over, he goes to the dock and looks across the water at the green light burning on Buchanan's dock; again Daisy has not come. Though Nick finally brings them together, there are too many cross-currents now for Gatsby and Daisy to make it back to one another; nor does Daisy's conscienceless flight after running over and killing a woman show her worthy. Yet to the end Gatsby stands by his incorruptible dream of her, and it is in this sense that Nick finds him cleaner than anyone. Nick has little use for "that most limited of all specialists, 'the well-rounded man'. This isn't just an epigram—life is much more successfully looked at from a single window, after all". It was precisely this narrow-ness of vision that Gatsby, the old sport in the pink suit, somehow preserved to the end. For Nick, drawn as he was to "the secret griefs of wild, unknown men", this was enough.

All sympathetic readers of *The Great Gatsby* cherish the intense perfection of scene in which this story occurs. Memorable are the cool wide lawns on summer evenings on the Island, certain hot, disagreeable hotel and tenement rooms in New York, and in between the unforgettable valley of ashes through which Gatsby races in his spectacular yellow car. One does not forget readily the ominous billboard advertising Dr. T. J. Eckleburg's Spectacles in that same valley: great blue eyes and yellow glasses a yard high, they watch and wait until, as it were, they compel to be enacted before them the devastating accident which maims all the lives of the book. It is part of the intensity of this short novel that this vale of ashes through which Nick and his friends pass so many times that summer is at once a 1922 highway, a corridor of hell, and a prophetic valley of decision. *The Great Gatsby* has the concentration and moral force of another fine book that came out a year later—Hemingway's *The Sun Also Rises*; they share a kind of stripped-down, lean perfection which I think Fitzgerald was never able to repeat, nor, for my taste, Hemingway either.

Was Fitzgerald a rebel? Yes, in that, born into a generation whose first delight was to purge itself of what it called 'puritanism' (meaning nineteenth- and not seventeenth-century morality), he became youth's spokesman for a new order; yes, in that sense. Or no, in the sense that, readily accepting the fashionable new ways, he found it hard to rebel against his own generation. And no, in that, when the 'thirties posed deep social problems for the writer, Fitzgerald stood apart, not so much choosing against such subject matter as finding himself unable to cope with it. But certainly there was private rebellion in his study of Gatsby, in the centre of whose illegality he exposed a vein of purity. Then and whenever else Fitzgerald put a higher price on art and insight than on survival, he joined the ranks of those who rebel by spending themselves without counting the cost. Fitzgerald was perfectly conservative, it seems to me, in his social attitudes; or rather he was not a social thinker at all in the harder sense of that term. Many of his stories are no more than commercial writings by a gifted reporter of his age. But when he could make himself do it, when he could jack himself up, when he could narrow his vision, when he could hold a paradox in his head though it hurt, as he did when he lined the decay of decent Dick Diver, when he could bring to his fiction something of Stahr's assurance that "I am the unity. I am the unity" —at these times he gave life and tragic power to the human comedy.

We expect of a novel that it present a story in a way that awakens our imagination as we read. We should also ask that in retrospect the story shall seem to have existed in a definable world of values—moral, social, psychological—peculiar to itself yet relevant to general human experience. This Fitzgerald could do, when he could keep that white sweater of his from being so much wool over the eyes. He came very close to mastering the idiom and rhythm of the American speech of his time, and the novelist who can do this has a most strategic resource at his command. We have to go to Hemingway or Ring Lardner or back to Mark Twain to match Fitzgerald's American cadences, or come forward to J. D. Salinger's *The Catcher in the Rye* (this is the book that that sounds nearest right to our latest younger generation).

Fitzgerald had, too, a whirling sensitivity to the moment of beauty, and though it is usually said that wealth was his subject, I have thought, reading him this time, that in a way it is only his medium and not his subject, the means by which he sets situations which allow him to work at the kind of values that interest him—the subtle give and take, the play, between men and women not otherwise occupied. It permitted him to get his range, as the choice of seventeenth-century settings did for Hawthorne. If Fitzgerald's most desperate need was for success of some sort, he also deeply craved to be a responsible artist. In a broken way he served the stern apprenticeship that this requires. He also felt a moral hunger, and although he did not have the head for intricate moral shadings he kept a desperate attachment to the play of values in his characters.

He was unsure, this boy wonder of the American 'twenties, a charming, insecure Adonis of a lad who never quite wanted to grow up and almost succeeded. He lacked the equipment for great art or great rebellion. Yet he had genuine talent, and his desperate ambition to make good resulted in three novels—*Gatsby* (all of it), *Tender is the Night* (parts of it), and *The Last Tycoon* (the fine sequence in chapters 3 and 4)—which are sure to haunt us for some time to come.

H. L. MENCKEN: CHANGELESS CRITIC
IN CHANGING TIMES

BY LEWIS LEARY

TIME HAS NOT BEEN KIND TO H. L. MENCKEN. THE terror of the 'twenties has become something of a period piece, embarrassingly a reminder of rejected taste, like an old sofa on which we wonder how we could ever have been comfortable. Its curious curls and furbelows are outrageously disproportioned. Even the lines which pleased us once as *svelte* and debonair are bumpy now with prejudice and wrong-headedness. The springs are sagging and the stuffing shows, so that we put it aside, no longer useful except as lumber stored for keepsake.

Yet hardly more than a quarter of a century ago and during the two decades of his ascendancy as editor of *The Smart Set* and then *The American Mercury*, Mencken provided a rallying point for the literature of protest in the United States. Every young man read him as surrogate for his own father, who was not so wise, and thrilled to what the Sage of Baltimore had to say of venality in the United States. With the sybaritic George Jean Nathan at his right hand and, finally, with Alfred A. Knopf substantially at his left, he dedicated himself, he said, to "the most noble and sublime task possible to mere human beings: the overthrow of superstition and unreasoning faith".

Like Bernard Shaw, whom he admired, he pampered the masochism of young America by beating it about the head until the ringing in its ears was interpreted as cerebration. So wanton were his strokes and so responsive his victims that the *New York Times* was soon to describe him as "the most powerful private citizen" in the United States. "If I had the power," said Sinclair Lewis, "I'd make Henry Mencken the Pope of America. He spreads the message of sophistication that we need so badly."

Sophistication was then a favourite word, and Mencken was fond of recalling evidences of it in his own family history. His forebears in Germany had included learned and iconoclastic professors at the University of Leipzig and sophisticated professional men, even one who had employed Johann Sebastian Bach as choirmaster. But Mencken's grandfather, who left the homeland in the turbulent 1840s, and then his father had become prosperous in the tobacco business in Baltimore, their sophistication diluted by baseball and beer. And young Henry was a bookworm who returned, he thought, to an older and better tradition, which would have none of trade. His appetite for books was large, and he wrote poetry. When he later recalled the days of his youth in autobiographical volumes, he called them *Happy Days*, *Newspaper Days*, and then *Heathen Days*. For books were finally to be no more satisfying than cigar-making. In his late teens he abandoned them, he said, "in favour of life itself". He became, that is, a newspaperman, then an editor, and finally an editorial commentator, and these he remained the rest of his days.

His comment was brisk, witty, and devastating. He was bumptious and unfair, and he stung even pious men to intemperate reply. In the verbal warfare which resulted Mencken was castigated as a wild-eyed, wide-mouthed jackass, a maggot, a ghoul, a bilious buffoon, a British toady, a super-Boche of German *Kultur*. But he gave as good as he received, and his barbs stuck. He was shocking, improper, and vulgar, raucous and unrepentant, and the tempo of intellectual life in America seemed quickened by his verbal pyrotechnics. No idol was safe, neither religion nor manners, and particularly not the idols of pretension.

During the years just before and just after the First World War the United States needed someone like H. L. Mencken to sting it from complacency, just as it needed Ezra Pound, Theodore Dreiser, and others among its rebels. "America," Robinson Jeffers was to write,

"settles in the mold of its vulgarity,
heavily thickening to empire,

And protest, only a bubble in the molten mass,
pops and sighs out, and the mass hardens."

Mencken's protest against America's perverse wrong-headedness, his championship of intellectual unrest, if even for its own sake, was something more than a bubble. His bellicose and pretentious extravagance was peculiarly American, and met an American need.

For the United States was settling in the mould of vulgarity during the early decades of the twentieth century. She had grown too fast and had not caught up with herself. The resources of the continent had been explored and exploited. The robber barons of the Gilded Age fattened on oil and coal and steel and corruption. Railroads spread their octopus arms throughout the land. Titles and castles and works of art were imported to reinforce the pretensions of the *nouveau riche*. Literature had become platitude. And hand in hand with the vulgarity of display went the not lesser vulgarity of reform, of provincial morality which found release in censorship, the prohibition of alcoholic beverages, and the eccentric notion that each man was in fact his brother's keeper.

Things of this kind inevitably breed revolt, and men like Mencken inevitably arise to lead the charge. What it is difficult for those of us who grew toward maturity under his spell to remember is that it was not really the bellicose Mr. Mencken who pulled the UnitedStates from the quagmire of self-satisfaction in which it then wallowed. His emergence as an intellectual force coincided almost exactly with the appearance during the second decade of the century of poetry by Pound and Eliot, Robert Frost, Carl Sandburg, Vachel Lindsay, and Wallace Stevens, and during the third decade of the century with the resurgence in fiction which brought forth Scott Fitzgerald, Hemingway, Dos Passos, Thomas Wolfe, and finally William Faulkner. It was people like these who created the real image, the abiding criticism, of contemporary America. Mencken was what we in the United States would call a cheer leader, an energetic man who bounds boisterously up and down on the sidelines, shouting encouragement, and inciting an almost mindless mob of spectators to roars of properly placed approval.

He was of an older generation than most of these others. Unable or too self-conscious seriously to create, he encouraged; criticism, he said, is the beating of a big drum, and that he did, and loudly. "What ails the beautiful letters of the Republic," said Mencken, "is what ails the general culture of the Republic—the lack of a body of sophisticated and civilised public opinion, independent of plutocratic control and superior to the infantile philosophies of the mob—a body of opinion showing the eager curiosity, the educated scepticism and hospitality of ideas of a true aristocracy." This was good and right, we thought, and better said than when Henry James or Fenimore Cooper or Brockden Brown had said it. We responded to it without recognising that it brought us little farther than we had been before. And Mencken, to whom we looked for guidance, stopped right there.

For behind his mask of pert ingenuousness, Mencken, bred in an age of pretension, was himself a pretentious man, proud in display of his mind or person. His weapon was the cudgel, and he practised its devastating, strong strokes before the mirror of contemporary approval. Superficially educated and writing faster than he learned, he was a man of few basic ideas, and even those who admired him most admit that many of them were absurd, others cheap or factitiously false. His was a simple Manichean universe of light and darkness, and the torch which he held in his pudgy hand was the light of the world. Like the Puritans whom he affected to despise, he was upheld by assurance of grace, and weighted with the burden of shaping an unregenerate people to his pattern.

His most effective writing has been described as a single, continuing harangue directed against things of which most of his countrymen were most proud: the efficacy of education, the sanctity of the home, the purity of marriage, love, religion, and the United States Supreme Court, children and obnoxious women without the "decency to keep quiet when their menfolk talk", and clergymen, because, he said, "the man of the cloth is *ipso facto* a fraud and to be watched especially when there are young girls or young boys around". His heavy club swept through a wide circle: "From the Boy Scouts, and from home cooking, from Odd Fellows' funerals, from Socialists and Christians—Good Lord, deliver us!" The harangue was smart and cheap, vulgar and invigorating. We were too young in rebellion to remember that the same things had been better said before.

"Blow the froth off Mencken," it has been suggested, "and you get Shaw; skim the scum off Shaw and you get Nietzsche; drain the lees and settlings of Nietzsche's melancholy brain and you get Schopenhauer." As a journalist and freelance writer of fiction at the turn of the century, Mencken had been attracted to the Irish iconoclast, on whom in 1905 he wrote what is said to be the first critical volume. From Shaw he was inevitably led to Nietzsche. "After that," he said, "I was a critic of ideas, and I have remained so ever since." But what kind of a critic? And of what ideas?

His book on *The Philosophy of Friedrich Nietzsche* in 1908 sketched the ground plan on which most of Mencken's subsequent notions were to be erected. The world was divided, we were there told, into two kinds of people, those who were congenitally superior and those who were congenitally inferior—those who were supermen and those who were slaves, those who were elect and those who were unregenerate. There they were, and there they remained. Mass education was a waste of money because the inferior could not be taught and the superior needed no teaching beyond what their superior, and inevitably wealthy, parents could provide. Public charity was to be avoided because the congenitally inferior mass was not worth saving. They were mongrel and mediocre people, incapable of spiritual aspiration. Religion was a ruse by which the weak attempted to reduce the strong to their level. Politics was a game for charlatans, and democracy was the worst possible form of government, the tool of "poltroons and mob masters": "All government, in its essence," he said, "is a conspiracy against the superior man; its one permanent object is to oppress and cripple him."

The climate of political opinion today has tempted some commentators to bow towards Mencken as one who was almost alone among his generation in resisting lip-service to the Marxist way, for socialism was to him simply democracy advanced from lunacy to madness. They speak of his "somewhat battered optimism", as if he were a piquant and perverse Carl Sandburg whose secret insistence was on "The People, Yes". Whatever his private sentiment, his public image of America was of "a horde of peasants incredibly enriched, and with almost infinite power thrust into their hands". It was a mindless mob, motivated by self-admiration and controlled by fear. It was on these that superior men could play.

Ideas like Mencken's have become distressingly familiar. They disturb us because they remind us of times, even of temporary commitments, which we are uncomfortable in remembering. We in the United States are continuingly disturbed because people like Westbrook Pegler or the late Senator McCarthy have championed ideas not greatly unsimilar. Mencken's espousal of them explains why he was called the Mussolini of American letters, why during both world wars he was avoided as pro-German because, at the same time that he ridiculed the goose-step or the Nazi salute, he spoke quizzically of the Kaiser or in sympathy with Hitler's programme for European conquest, and why, finally, he was embarrassed to meet Ezra Pound in St. Elizabeth's Hospital in Washington, where the poet was incarcerated because he had spoken openly of matters about which Mencken during the 1940s was studiously silent.

Something of a similar embarrassment confuses us who admired him in the 1920s and who find the after-taste of Mencken unpleasant today. We remind ourselves that he was a poseur, that his tongue was more blunt than his mind, that his heart, we say, was in the right place. We recall that his genius was for hyperbole, that his method was that of shock, that he was a gadfly who stung us towards thinking. He ridiculed our fathers' gods, he

pointed derisively at our own inherited deficiencies, and
in his often simulated and pretentious wrath seemed
genuinely funny in the tradition he had learned from
Mark Twain and the exaggerations of frontier humour.
And we laughed.

But the fun was of the surface, and the surface was
kaleidoscope. He posed as an irascible and ribald Teu-
tonic god. The world of ideas, we have been told, was
his bowling alley, and he toppled the props of our
innocence with his chattering verbiage. His seemed so
refreshing, so necessary a voice. The targets of his rage
were progressives, prim novelists who made the desert of
American fiction at once so populated and so dreary, vice
crusaders, patriots, osteopaths, Methodists and Baptists and
Christian Scientists (and, not always for the same reasons,
Jews), the anti-saloon league, and American women "who
were full of Peruna and as fecund as the shad". He derided
Woodrow Wilson's League of Nations and Franklin
Roosevelt's New Deal. He considered the Library
of Congress under the direction of Archibald MacLeish
a Communist propaganda agency. Social reform of any
kind was repulsive to him, or any of "the bilge of
idealism" which runs in American veins: "A good
politician," he said, "is quite as unthinkable as an honest
burglar." H. G. Wells should have stuck to fiction rather
than attempt to remake the world. Even Shaw, once
admired, was finally dismissed as the 'Ulster Polonius', a
windbag blown large with platitudes: "it was his life work
to announce the obvious in terms of the scandalous".

The temptation is to dismiss Mencken with the same glib aphorism. But Mencken is not easily dismissed, and we hold tentatively to our admiration for him, not because of his view of the world or his estimate of its literature, but for two things besides: his championship of the right of any author to freedom of honest expression and his vitalising effect, as writer and as lexicographer, on the American language.

His part in the great American Battle of the Books, when he defended Dreiser, Sinclair Lewis, Sherwood Anderson, and others who would write realistically of the world as they saw it, places us with only few reservations greatly in his debt. He was on the right side, whatever his reasons, and his impudent diatribes against genteel critics, some of them ultimately more right but less vigorous than he, undoubtedly did smooth the way for better novelists, like Hemingway and Faulkner. But even in this he was a man of his time, effectively expressing convictions which many of his less articulate or strategically less well placed contemporaries held as strongly. It is difficult from this distance to assess the situation clearly, but it seems reasonable to suppose that we should have proceeded quite as far without him. One is even tempted by the notion that his bluntness may have done us harm, for it forced us to assumptions about the relation of realism to literature which quieter thinking has tempted us to put aside.

In our present perhaps equally perverse but more analytical mood, we suspect that Mencken was in no genuine sense a critic of literature at all. He was a moralist, a sociologist with a blistering vocabulary. The function of criticism, he said, was to lunge about right and left in vigorous strokes which knock the reigning idols off their perches. As editor, his measure for acceptance was often the inability of an author to find publication elsewhere. He never really admired or understood James Joyce, but he printed him when few else would: it was symbol of his protest. Dreiser was "flaccid, elephantine, doltish, coarse, dismal, flatulent", but Dreiser was worth championing because, like Sinclair Lewis and Ben Hecht, he exposed the scandalous shortcomings of the "boobs, dupes, and lackies" of America. People like James Branch Cabell and Joseph Hergesheimer were excellent because they wrote with "the artless and super-abundant energy of little children" in producing "a faithful reflection of national life . . . more faithful in its defects . . . than in its merits". He liked the early Willa Cather for the same reasons, but he virtually ignored Henry James, Edith Wharton, Ellen Glasgow, Stephen Crane, and (strangely) Frank Norris. He responded with little enthusiasm to the post-war fiction of Hemingway, Dos Passos, or Faulkner. George Ade was a great humorist, Ring Lardner was not. "The purpose of novel writing, as that crime is committed in the United States," he said, "is not to interpret life but to varnish, veil and perfume life—to make it a merry round of automobiling, country-clubbing, seduction, money-making and honeymooning, with music by Victor Herbert."

One does not prove a man no critic by this touchstone method in reverse. Mencken had standards. We are reminded that he introduced a whole generation to Hermann Sudermann, Maeterlinck, Sainte-Beuve, and, at one remove, Ibsen. He flaunted his standards: "I am by nature a vulgar fellow. I prefer *Tom Jones* to *The Rosary*, *Rabelais* to the Elsie books. . . . I delight in beef stews, limericks, and burlesque shows. When the mercury is above ninety-five I dine in my shirt sleeves and write poetry naked." He did not necessarily mean a compliment to Lizette Reese when he said that she wrote more genuine poetry than all the new poets put together, and he said something teasingly acute when he called Robert Frost a Whittier without whiskers. But his standards were not literary standards, nor were they moral in the sense that Lionel Trilling has used the term. They were derivative, stubbornly partisan, and more than often wrong. He struck about him with demonic glee, as enraptured as we by the fresh vigour of his vocabulary, and how the heads did roll.

Whether he wrote it naked or not, Mencken had no patience with poetry, even his own, which was of the self-consciously humorous kind which approaches a subject seriously but then backs off with an embarrassed quip at what it was about to say. "Women, damaged men, and others who are ill at ease in the world of sound ideas," he said, "write poetry." It was a little un-American, unless written as Sandburg or Lindsay wrote it. He relegated the Nashville Fugitives to "the Fringes of Lovely Letters", because they "tried to detach themselves from the ordinary flow of American ideas and convert themselves into an intellectual aristocracy"—by which he meant an intellectual aristocracy other than his own. Eliot and Pound were foetal poets, perversely un-American. Exceptions were made for Poe and Whitman because they dared swim against the tide, but he found even Poe sometimes ridiculous, and sponsored an article on Whitman as a rhymer of not even the second class, but only a word-monger and general phoney—a judgment to which he did not subscribe but which he was eager to present because, he explained, "I think we ought to get the professors sore. For years they said Whitman was a bum, now they say he's an angel. Let's keep them hopping and squirming."

If Mencken was neither an original thinker nor a critic, he was an excellent journalist, with an eye on circulation, and he became also a sociologist who amused himself with collecting material on the folkways of the United States. Not the least of these were idiosyncrasies of American speech, curious examples of which he had filed away for many years. When during the First World War he found it good sense to be quiet, he turned to his notes and put together the first edition of his giant study of *The American Language* which pointed to "salient differences between the English of England and the English of America as practically written and spoken—differences in vocabulary, in syntax, in grammar".

The impact of the book was immediate and large. "Never," said the reviewers, "has the flourishing personality of H. L. Mencken been so happily exercised." His biographer tells us that "with one powerful stroke he hewed in half the umbilical cord which philologically bound the nation to England". There were protests, of course, that Mencken, an Anglophobe and no patriot, attempted to "split asunder the two great English-speaking peoples", but the book, conceived as an innocuous avocation during troubled times and described by its compiler as "a heavy indigestible piece of cottage cheese", sold amazingly well.

And it is probably this book, which has gone through four editions and to which two large supplements have been added, for which Mencken, even against his protest, will be remembered. "I have never been a scholar and have never pretended to be one," he scolded. "I am just a scout for scholars. I accumulated the material and tried to put it in readable form, so people could understand it, and dug out of it whatever human juices there were, and there were plenty, and my hope and idea was that the material I had accumulated would be used by actual philologists." It has been used, and with gratitude, even by philologists who dismiss it as "an elephantine newspaper story".

It is a catch-all and it does sprawl, but here finally was a sedate and serious, even a humble, Mencken, different indeed from the man who during these same war years wrote a pert volume *In Defense of Women* which put forward the not incredible theory that wives are more competent than their husbands, who, beneath a noisy play at efficiency, are really nincompoops with shoddy souls: "A man's women folk, whatever their outward show of respect for his merit and authority, always regard him secretly as an ass, and with something akin to pity." But women should remain women, and stay out of trousers. How ridiculous they looked in uniform: "like a dumb-bell run over by an express train. Below the neck by the bow and below the waist astern there are two masses that simply refuse to fit into a balanced composition."

We are tempted to believe that behind Mencken's bellicose exterior lurked a gentler soul, easily shocked. The post-war freedom of America, especially of American women, saddened him. The most virtuous of lady novelists wrote things which would make a bartender blush: "When I began reviewing," he said, "I used to send my review copies, after I had sweated through them, to the Y.M.C.A. Now I send them to the medical college." Night-clubs saddened him also. They were filled with "middle-aged couples bumping and grunting over the dance floor like dying hogs in a miasmic pen". He detested the radio, Hollywood, and literary cocktail parties. Yet he found himself and enjoyed himself as spokesman for just the people who created and patronised these things. He ridiculed scoutmasters and clergymen as delayed adolescents, their brains so flooded with poisons of piety that there was no room for thinking. But Mencken was really the most adolescent of them all. It was wonderful sport, he thought, to steal Gideon Bibles from hotels and send them to his friends inscribed as from the author. When a neighbour complained that his wood-pile was unsightly, Mencken soberly painted it in gaudy colours. Nothing was more fun than to borrow a friend's distinctively styled automobile and park it conspicuously in front of some notorious bordello.

How then is it possible to take a man of this kind seriously? Yet we did, and we do. His principal vocation was supplying sharp new teeth to old saws, like the one which describes love as the illusion that one woman differs from another. His technique was of shock and surprise. His protest was for protest's sake, and he could not resist a quip even when directed against something which he had formerly defended when the words sounded better that way. It has been said in his defence that he spoke always in a state of frenzy, and that the "frenzy was generally the frenzy of love, love of America and of its history and traditions, people and customs, heroes and rogues, saints and sinners and clowns . . . glories and aberrations, and dreams and hopes and regrets and miseries and—all that is America".

He loved life, that is to say, and had an avid appetite for it. He wished, he said, that he might attain the "worldly wisdom of a police lieutenant, a bartender, a shyster lawyer, and a midwife". And this he may be supposed to have done—he policed his constituents with ruthless power; he intoxicated with attractive strong words; as shyster, he befuddled us with half-truths; and sometimes he presided over the birth of an idea, not the less precious because he had not fathered it but only held it by its heels and slapped it hard so that other men might hear its voice. Love of life and of ideas are admirable things, and love which reacts in angry protest against unnecessary deficiencies in life as it is lived in one's country is admir-

able also. But to say that Mencken served a purpose is
not to say that he was a great or admirable man. He has
been compared, with what justice I do not know, with
Malcolm Muggeridge. He has been compared also with
Juvenal, Dryden, Swift, Voltaire, Ambrose Bierce, and
Philip Wylie, but the favourite comparison among his
admirers today is with Dr. Johnson. His biographer
invites us to consider the obvious parallels:

"They were both periodical essayists, both popular
critics. Each became famous as a literary dictator,
though neither was in fact any such thing. Both were
lexicographers who worked under immense handicaps,
yet neither of them had more than scant regard for his
lexicography. Each professed Toryism loudly yet pre-
ferred the residue of humanity to its froth. . . . They
were boyhood prodigies who all their lives looked
back upon their schooldays as the happiest of their
lives. Each was the eldest son of a tradesman who
impressed him into the family business against his will.
Each received a limited formal education, educated
himself irregularly, and had small regard for the lecture
platform. . . . Each believed mankind happier in a
state of subordination and endeavored to put all men
who entered his company in that situation. Each was
a lover of good food and drink, of earnest conversation
with men and playful banter with women, and neither
could talk unless he could dominate the conversation.
Neither believed that there were two sides to any
question; both served as parlor conservatives in

periods when the left was advancing; each could be
outrageously sophistic; each could be terribly wrong.
Both admired the city extravagantly and despised the
provinces. For Johnson it was Scotland; for Mencken
the plains of 'sunbaked, unwashed Kansas'. Johnson,
an Englishman, hated America; Mencken, an American,
hated England. They were gargantuans both, wits
both, neurotics both—the one a feeler of lamp-posts;
the other an inveterate scrubber of hands. . . . Each
was hard on incompetence, stern with cant, brutal with
dishonesty."

The capacity of each for work and anger seems to have
been unlimited, and each mirrored some of the virtues
and many of the shortcomings of his age. If such a comparison as I have quoted in outline seems meretricious,
perhaps that speaks also of shortcomings which we who
admired him have inherited. In Mencken, these included
lack of candour, limitation of intellectual equipment or,
at best, its misuse, and an inability to respond to the
aspiring spirit of man with anything more than embarrassment which retreats to derision. Victimised by
journalism, which Henry James once described as "so
pervasive, so ubiquitous, so unprecedentedly prosperous,
so wonderful for outward agility, but so unfavorable,
even so fatal, to development from within", Mencken
made shoddy use of his talent for language. He was not
as wise, nor was he as perverse, as Ezra Pound. He had
some of the traits but few of the submissive virtues of
Henry Thoreau. It is not his vulgarity that we resent, his

writing in shirt-sleeves or his great belly laughs—we are used to those. We admire something much like them in Mark Twain and Walt Whitman, whom Mencken admired also.

It comes, then, with something of a shock that no better words are found for summing up this retrospective view of Mencken than those which Henry James used almost a hundred years ago in talking about Walt Whitman. "We look in vain . . . for a single idea. We find nothing but flashy imitations of ideas." Things which we have learned to look upon as faulty because man is faulty, but which are human and therefore good, are "sneered at on every page, and nothing positive given us in their place". We still admire the sparks which Mencken gave off and wish some of them had quickened to fire. There was grit in him and resonance. He could have been a good reflector, making magic with words like Whitman and Pound, and that might have been enough. What destroyed him was pretension. "To be positive," Henry James continues, "one must have something to say; to be positive requires reason, labor and art; and art requires, above all things, a suppression of one's self, a subordination of one's self to an idea."

This Mencken could not do. That is one of the reasons why, as he pointed like an irascible schoolmaster to the iniquitous shortcomings of the "ordinary, dreary, sweating, struggling people", and the mountebanks, sharpers, and coney-catchers of his generation, there was something distinctively American about H. L. Mencken. Not in his ideas, which were from the ragbag of European thought, but in his use of them as sticking-plasters to mend the mind and manners of men. As moralist, he was opportunist, striking at the manifestation rather than at the root, at the form rather than the substance. He led us, we can say, towards the brink with no sure knowledge of what lay beyond. Like Sinclair Lewis and Scott Fitzgerald, whom he admired or disliked for the wrong reasons, he was finally as much symptom as corrective of the maladies he would mend. We stomped and we snorted to the rhythms which he beat, so busily engaged that we had no time to notice that the mirror he held up to his time was so steamed over by the force of his breath upon it that it concealed as much as it reflected.

Perhaps we are wrong to expect more than titillation from young rebels, whose traditional function has been to disturb rather than create, but I find Mencken in strange company in this series which begins so well with Thoreau and ends so provocatively with Faulkner. I should have expected to find within it such men as Emerson, our great focus of revolt, or Melville, who dared the peril of diving deeply; George Santayana, whose heart, he said, did in truth rebel against his generation, might be there, and even Ezra Pound, though his later protest grew shrill with monomania. Yet when we ask which are more representative of protest in the United States, the men who form the body of this series or the wiser men who dared tentativeness and profundity, we are saddened by the wisdom which planned the series so well. We recognise our American rebels as journeymen, content with patchwork repairs, shrill, self-pitying or self-congratulatory, themselves finally the product of their own rhetoric. Whatever their achievement, collectively or singly, they have failed us by representing us so well.

But when we are tired, Mencken sometimes reassures us still. One of the last things he wrote before he was incapacitated by illness was a credo which said in part: "Today no decent value in all the scale of human values is safe, and neither is any decent man"; yet "intelligence is at work all the while, though from time to time it must go underground. Let us hope that it will emerge more anon, and pull the reluctant human race along another peg." In this hope, I think, we join him.

JOHN STEINBECK:
THE FITFUL DAEMON

BY R. W. B. LEWIS

STEINBECK'S LITERARY REPUTATION IS NOT VERY HIGH at the moment and I see few reasons why it should grow greater in the future. It has declined a good deal since its peak during the war years. Following the publication of his most determined novel, *The Grapes of Wrath*, in 1939, it declined in America, where Steinbeck had for some years exerted a strong but as it were non-literary, and hence non-durable, appeal. And it declined in Europe, where he had been confusedly but advantageously associated with writers like Hemingway and Faulkner, with whom Steinbeck has little in common, and with writers like Dos Passos and Thomas Wolfe, whom he has at times perhaps superficially resembled. The prestige of that entire hydra-headed beast, the American novelist, has diminished notably in Europe, and the Steinbeck-head of it as much as any.

At the same time, Steinbeck is no doubt in some vague way established as a novelist. I see that a university press is bringing out a doctoral dissertation on Steinbeck's fiction, and a volume of critical essays about him by several hands has made its appearance. Thus he has been accorded the respectful burial which is our contemporary American way of honouring living writers whom we have pretty well decided not to read any longer. The decision is perhaps unfortunate and even unfair, but it is not altogether unreasonable. There is a sense of promise unfulfilled in Steinbeck's writing over the past decade and a half. His career is something of a casualty, and a casualty I think in this particular case of an unlucky wedding between art and rebellion which developed into a fatal marital hostility between the poetic and the political impulse. His career to date has the shape of a suggestive, a representative, and a completely honourable failure.

If, as Faulkner has rather perversely contended, a writer is to be measured these days by the extent and quality of his failure, Steinbeck must inevitably be reckoned among our most sizeable novelists. Steinbeck's failure is great, and it is incomparably more interesting and valuable than the successes of nine-tenths of his contemporaries. For where Steinbeck has failed is in an effort to engage, with the resources of fiction, the complex realities, the evolving motifs, the outlines and images of things, the very sense of life which make up the matter truly, if deeply and almost invisibly, available to an American novelist of his generation. I am not cheaply hinting that Steinbeck deserves, as the schoolboy saying goes, 'E' for effort. I am saying that because of his effort and even because of its failure he has made more visible for the rest of us the existence, indeed the precise character, of the realities and themes and images he has not finally succeeded in engaging. This is the kind of failure which is, in the end, almost indistinguishable from success, though we may not be sure where to catalogue it; whether, for example, under the heading of literature or of criticism, of art or of history.

Amidst the larger failure of Steinbeck there are smaller units of undeniable achievement. At least one of these comprises a whole brief story; more usually the achievement is partial—a passage, a character, or perhaps merely an aspect. *Of Mice and Men* (1937) seems on a re-reading to stand up remarkably well, to stand up whole and intact. It skirts breathtakingly close to disastrous sentimentality; stock minor characters (especially the villain and the villainess) move woodenly through it; the deliberate stage technique gives one the cramps; and there is an unpersuasive quality of contrivance about the episode—the mercy-shooting of an aged dog—which prepares by analogy for the climax—the mercy-shooting of the animal-child, Lennie. Yet the entire action of the story moves to its own rhythm, rescued and redeemed by a sort of wistful toughness, a sense not of realism but of reality. The end is an authentic purgation of feeling, pity if not terror, and the end crowns the whole.

Of Mice and Men is probably the only one of Steinbeck's works which is satisfying as a whole, and it is a short novel or *novella*. His longer and thicker writings may be differentiated by the moment and degree of wreckage, and they have culminated in *East of Eden* (1952), professedly Steinbeck's most ambitious novel. "Nearly everything I have is in it," he said. I am afraid it is a very bad novel of a very special and revealing badness which can most quickly be described by saying that it would have been greatly admired by the late H. G. Wells, who referred to Steinbeck as "that amazing genius".

The badness of *East of Eden* is a basic premise in this paper and I must return to it, but meanwhile a couple of observations of a less negative kind. The sheer bulk of

Steinbeck's work is impressive, for one thing, and marks him clearly as a professional of sorts: twenty-three volumes, some of them no doubt slim ones, in the twenty-six years following his first book, *The Cup of Gold*, in 1929. Bulk is not the first attribute of artistic achievement, but it is *an* attribute, and we note again the courage and resiliency which are part of Steinbeck's temperament, which set him apart from the 'signers-off' of contemporary fiction, with their tender brevities and their lamentations about the plight of the artist, and which permit him to continue in the face of what must surely be for Steinbeck periodic frustration.

More important, and secondly, in the longer novels (*To a God Unknown*, 1933, *In Dubious Battle*, 1936, *The Grapes of Wrath*, 1939, and *East of Eden*) we come upon electrifying passages, sudden and tragically short-lived moments of vision, little spurts of verbal energy; momentary manifestations, as it were, of a trapped and imprisoned artistic daemon struggling to get out and on to the page and into the language, and to dwell there for ever. We come upon an occasional character too who lights up for us the adventure he is engaged in: normally not the hero—not Joseph Wayne or Tom Joad or Jim Nolan or Adam Trask—but the Steinbeck sage, the renegade doctor or renegade minister or renegade philosopher, whose puzzled involvement with the action helps to give the action such force and meaning as it may possess.

More largely yet, through these swift moments of light and these infrequent bearers of light, we dimly detect in these novels the effective presence and the design of the realities, motifs and images I have mentioned earlier. I distinguish here two kinds of motif in the fiction of John Steinbeck. The first may be called the American motif: a celebrational sense of *life*, a sense of promise and possibility and of as yet unspoiled novelty in man and his habitation, a mystical sympathy both for the individual and for what Whitman called the 'en-masse'. In short, a vision, if that is not too rarefied and romantic a word for it, which was of New England and the American east in its nineteenth-century origins and which Steinbeck has— I think very properly—naturalised in his native California and translated into its idiom.

The second is the contemporary motif: something so close in substance to the American motif that it can be seen as growing organically out of it, and yet which also appears as a dominant motif in the fiction of other contemporary languages and countries. In appears in the fiction, for example, of Silone in Italy, of Malraux and Camus in France, and to some extent of Graham Greene in England. This motif springs from the tragic awareness, which in Steinbeck's case is sometimes only an intensely pathetic awareness, of the fateful division between man and man; and of that division as a central feature of the mutilated life it is the novelist's business to give a direct impression.

The sense of division leads naturally to the political theme. It leads, that is, to the intuition that the form which the human struggle currently assumes, the representative plot of contemporary experience and the soul of its tragedy, is political in design. The political theme consists of a revolt against the forces that keep men separated, and its heart tends to beat to the formula of Albert Camus: I rebel, therefore we are. Or it pulses yet more movingly to the rhythm suggested by Ignazio Silone: "What determined my rebellion was the choice of companions."

Steinbeck has made his contribution to the theme and its heart-beat, especially in *The Grapes of Wrath*. "This is the beginning," he says there, flatly, in his own voice, "from 'I' to 'we'." But the relation between the elements —the felt division, the rebellion, and the ordering power of art—is extremely complex. It is partly Steinbeck's habit of over-simplifying both life and art that has kept him from seeing and taking hold of the complex entirety. The elements rarely fuse in his fiction; they tend rather to jar against each other. The same may be said of the two leading motifs. The evolution of what I have named the contemporary motif from the American motif may be seen within the development of American literature itself, in the movement from Thoreau and Emerson to Hawthorne and from all of them to Henry James; a movement from the happy evocation of "the simple separate person" and the sturdy conviction that the world was, or could be seen as, young and uncorrupted, to the gradual sense of self-isolation, of darkness and bewilderment. And thence to the ensuing perception that the form of human experience was exactly the strenuous, perhaps desperate, need and effort of separated individuals to draw close to one another, to enjoy an experience of life by means of a human relationship, in what Henry James was to call "the great greasy sea" of the anarchic modern world.

There is no such coherent and meaningful evolution in Steinbeck's work, though he began reasonably enough in the recognisably American vein and has gone on to identify, and respond boldly to, the contemporary challenge. The motifs have not so much met together as collided, in a struggle, as it were, between poetry and politics. For Steinbeck's poetry, the truly creative side of him, has remained American while his engrossing theme has become contemporary and political. As it turns out it has been the poetry which has suffered, which is simply a way of referring again to Steinbeck's intermittent novelistic achievement. Maybe the sacrifice was beneficial. Steinbeck's gallant effort and his honourable defeat can remind us how huge an enterprise it is to make known the results of seeking.

The American theme announces itself regularly in Steinbeck's stories in a recurring image of a sort of *Drang nach Westen*—or perhaps *Drang nach* California. Steinbeck's first novel, *To a God Unknown*, begins with the departure of Joseph Wayne, the book's indistinctly godlike hero, from the family home in New England, near Pittsford, Vermont, to the green hills of California. "I've been reading about the West and the good cheap land there," he tells his father; "I've a hunger for the land, sir." "It's not just restlessness," his father replies. "You may go to the West. You are finished here with me." The process is repeated, through dialogue rather less

stagey, in *East of Eden*, when Adam Trask leaves his
Connecticut home and heads for California. "It's nice
there, sun all the time and beautiful." And the Joad
family in *The Grapes of Wrath*, though starting much
farther west, in Oklahoma, similarly sets off for the
Pacific coast not only to find work and a place to live
but to find a new world of hope and opportunity after
the hideous destruction of their old world.

Steinbeck's instinct at these initial moments was altogether sound; he was knowingly possessing himself of a
native theme and a native resource, a resource both of
history and of literature. It is the traditional American
impulse to withdraw into the terrain of freedom in order
to find or re-find one's identity and one's purpose as a
human being; to dissociate from the given, the orthodox,
the habitual, from whatever passes at the time for civilisa-
tion. "Aunt Polly she's going to . . . civilise me, and I
can't stand it. I been there before," Huck Finn says on
the last page of his memoirs. He determines accordingly
to "light out for the territories". The same impulse, of
course, received its most eloquent treatment in the
recorded withdrawal of Henry David Thoreau from the
quiet desperation of civilised Concord to the unfallen
nature and fertile solitude of Walden Pond, a few miles
away. But we remember also Cooper's Natty Bumppo
lighting out for the uncomplicated forest from the
oppressive society of the town of Templeton, and
Herman Melville, in fact and fiction, jumping ship to
reflect unfavourably upon the evils of civilisation from
the Eden-atmosphere of the Taipi valley in the South

Seas. Such was the form that rebellion originally took in American literature.

But in seeing his native Salinas Valley in California as a new Eden, the scene of a new chance for man and for men, and in transporting his heroes thither from the exhausted East, Steinbeck is not only continuing in an American tradition, enacting again an old American dream. He is also suggesting that the dream itself has moved west and has settled there, that it is now California which stimulates in its inhabitants the intoxicating sense of fresh beginnings and untroubled potentialities which the eastern scene once stimulated in Emerson, in Thoreau, in Whitman. This is the point and purpose of the prefatory incantations of *East of Eden*, where the local California countryside is observed and named as though by the first man at the dawn of time.

Much of the best and no little of the worst can be found in Steinbeck's work, and most apparently in the work of the early 'thirties—*The Pastures of Heaven, To a God Unknown*, and *Tortilla Flat*—where there are many parallels and continuities linking him to the age of Emerson and its cultural predispositions. Steinbeck really did, for example, write about those subjects Emerson urged on his contemporaries, when he suggested the range of native materials and the unsophisticated but robust activities ready to be celebrated: "Our log-rolling, our stumps and their politics, our fisheries, our Negroes and Indians, our boasts and our repudiations, the wrath of rogues and the pusillanimity of honest men, the northern trade, the southern planting, the western clear-

ing, Orgeon and Texas, are yet unsung." And in trans-
lating these persons and places and occupations into
narrative, Steinbeck managed to shed over all of it a
warm, in fact a slightly sweaty, haze of trustful moral
purity. Innocent are these early writings, and he who
wrote them; innocent in the manner of Emerson and
Thoreau; innocent in the manner of Whitman, detecting
or claiming to detect beauty and purity amidst the
lowliest squalor. There is no vice in the inhabitants of the
heavenly pastures; its liars and lunatics and killers and
prostitutes are merely well-intentioned eccentrics.

Joseph Wayne, in *To a God Unknown*, is so thickly
enveloped in mythological fog that he scarcely seems to
arrive at humanity at all. *To a God Unknown*, for all its
artificial loftiness, is perhaps the most promising of these
early books, but it has the severe literary—that is,
novelistic—defect of a protagonist who is so primal a
figure that he never takes on the burden of becoming
human, never enters into or is affected by the maturing
pressures of time.

Joseph Wayne is a representative character, for the fact
is that most of these early creations are morally pure
because they are morally as yet unborn. Joseph is
physically vigorous and his eyes have seen the glory.
With his vague, mystical far-sightedness, he is a sort of
buckskin Bronson Alcott, but he shares with the antic
trouble-makers of the other books the quality—in them
often very attractive—of pre-moral sensibility. None of
these persons has yet arrived at the condition of conscience,
at the human condition, and with luck none of them ever

will. Joseph's pre-moral, pre-historical profile seems an act of will. Following a traditional American pattern, Joseph has abandoned a closed or closing society. He has withdrawn westwards to commune in solitude with untainted nature and to listen for its secret. That, to repeat, is the form the rebellious impulse has so often taken in America—not a direct assault from within upon an intolerable social order or disorder, but a removal of the self with the aim of experiencing again the graceful simplicity by which society may be measured and from which society has gravely, but perhaps not hopelessly or irretrievably, fallen. It is a matter of tasting once more of the tree of ignorance and the interest of the story lies in what the refreshed hero can later make out of his wilderness adventure. For the next phase, in American literature, has customarily been the return into society to testify amidst its betrayals and denials to the lessons learned in solitude. Joseph Wayne does not live to make that return journey, but it is a sign of John Steinbeck's development that the role of the returned witness is exactly the one assigned, in *The Grapes of Wrath*, to Jim Casy, the one-time preacher who abruptly quits his vocation—"an' went off by myself an' give her a damn good thinkin' about"—and who has now come back to counsel Tom Joad and his family, and finally to die for the new faith that his good thinking had produced.

One of the favourite images by which American writers have traditionally sought both to describe and to comment on the process I have mentioned is the image of Adam. Such is the case with John Steinbeck and *East of*

Eden, his longest novel, in which the author put "nearly everything I have . . . pain and excitement . . . and feeling good or bad and evil thoughts and good thoughts—the pleasure of design and some despair and the indescribable joy of creation". This is a novel whose allegorical framework is indicated not only in its title but in its hero, whose Christian name is Adam. This is a novel which introduces us not only to a new Adam, but to a new Lilith and even to a new Cain and Abel—called Cal and Aron—with the former again responsible, if indirectly, for the death of the latter. And this is a novel whose characters spend many hours arguing the meaning of the Genesis story—"the best-known story in the world", as one of them says, "because it is everybody's story . . . the symbol story of the human soul".

Here, then, is the book in which Steinbeck has presented the whole of his experience of America. Although it has been a huge economic success, it is, unhappily, a literary disaster, and of such proportions that it sheds a very disturbing light on the career that has allegedly culminated in it. Either Steinbeck has not understood the original story of Adam or he has failed to grasp its profound relevance to experience in America: which is not to understand America itself. The story of Adam is the story of the fall of man. There are many mysteries about it, but there is no questioning the fact that it is a story about sin, about the encounter with evil and the corruption of human nature by an act of its own will and an expression of its pride. It is indeed the story of human nature *becoming* human, of someone less than or more than or other than human taking upon himself the tainted, paradoxical, tragic, and hopeful burden of authentic humanity; it is therefore about what it means to be human. It is a story about death, and a story which has always appealed to the characteristic dark humour of the American novelist. For its content is so well suited to suggest the maturing calamities which can befall the American Adam, neglectful of sin and evil, uninterested in paradox and impatient with tragedy, which he too often confuses with gloom.

Little of that old story remains in *East of Eden* and nothing of its inner essence. Adam Trask grows up in the East, some ninety years ago, marries a purportedly very bad woman named Cathy, takes her to California, where she leaves him and sets up as a madam in a bordello— after giving Adam twin boys. He engages in various enterprises, among them long and instructive conversations with his philosophical Chinese servant, and grows old among an assortment of family tribulations.

The biblical allegory is the more intrusive throughout this jumbled tale because the allegory has remained un- fleshed. Failing to represent the case, Steinbeck has attempted to name it. This gives rise to a pervasive sense of contrivance and we are conscious everywhere not of a sense of life but of an abstraction from it. The Bible story is about evil and in few novels has the word 'evil' been invoked as frequently as it is in *East of Eden*, but that itself is an evil sign. Moreover, Cathy, the alleged em- bodiment of evil, is revealingly defined as a moral freak, a preposterous deviation from human nature, rather than an aggravated and disturbing instance of its congenital tendencies. She strikes us at last as altogether unreal, a very naughty girl in some fable or ballad, the little girl, perhaps, who gave her father forty whacks.

There is no great image of human experience in *East of Eden* though a great one was intended, and not only because there is no sense of life but even more because there is no sense of death in it. Death is almost always the end of experience in Steinbeck, and the end of his characteristic fictions; it is almost never a beginning, never a dying into life. The fact is that Steinbeck does not really believe in his Biblical story. It is as though Emerson had written the book, and all that remains when the abstractions and monsters have been cleared away is the old Emersonian material and the old Emersonian tone: "the northern trade, the southern planting, the western clearing", and so on.

But the calamity which is *East of Eden* is partly explained by what had happened to Steinbeck's subject-matter and his attitude towards it in the years between those earlier and funnier and more cheerful works and the decision, say around 1950, to tackle the Adamic allegory. These were the years of observed human misery, of protest and rebellion, of *The Grapes of Wrath*.

Steinbeck's editor, Pascal Covici, has accurately noted in Steinbeck "an expression of the joy of living". It should be remembered here that by communicating that joy Steinbeck has given very many people a great deal of pleasure, revived in them perhaps some lost sense of the sheer excitement of being alive. And I cannot resist adding personally that behind his stories I detect a figure who is to me altogether sympathetic; a person of zest and humour and nervous anger, and with an uncommonly large fund of humanity. The difficulty with Steinbeck's peculiar brand of joyfulness is not so much that it can easily turn fuzzy or mawkish (a kind of melting process observable in the development, or the decline, from *Tortilla Flat* to *Cannery Row* and *Sweet Thursday*). The difficulty is rather that it is constitutionally unequipped to deal with the more sombre reality a man must come up against, in these times or in any times, if he is honest and alert.

Steinbeck was up against a part of that reality during the years between 1936 and 1942 when he was writing *In Dubious Battle*, *The Grapes of Wrath* and *The Moon is Down*, and when he was also writing the one work in which his trapped daemon did squirm out and get almost completely into the language—*Of Mice and Men*. With the important exception of the latter, the work of those years is characterised among other things by a seeming refusal, or perhaps an inability, to confront tragic truth. The result of having done so might have been a considerable enlargement of Steinbeck's art; the transformation, for instance, of the earlier earthy humour into what Hawthorne once called "the tragic power of laughter".

But the work of those years was characterised, too, by a relatively superficial analysis and a makeshift solution of the case, whether it be social injustice or Fascist invasion and oppression. To have looked more searchingly into those ugly phenomena would have been to have dis-

covered their tragic implications for the nature of man—
the proper concern, I venture, of the artist if not of the
politician or the sociologist. *The Moon is Down*, for
example, is intended as a consoling image of heroism—
that of a number of European villagers in a town occupied
by the Nazi forces. But it is woefully limited by the
absence of anything but the slightest hint that the fault,
the guilt, the very Fascism, is a manifestation of the human
heart, and so detectable on all sides of the conflict. Steinbeck typically permits a portion of goodness to modify
the badness of some of the invaders—especially the com-
manding officer, the book's one interesting characterisation—but none of the invaders' badness is reflected in the
hearts of the staunch and faithful villagers. Be good,
sweet maids and men, Steinbeck seems to be telling them,
and let who will be Fascist.

I am not now raising the somewhat tired issue of the
artist's responsibility. I am sure that responsibility is a
great one, but I am talking about the form it can most
suitably and effectively take—and that is the prophetic
form, penetrating to hidden realities and not combing up
appearances. Neither *The Grapes of Wrath* nor *In Dubious
Battle*, the novels where Steinbeck's rebellious sympathy
for the wretched and the luckless is most evident, succeeds in arriving at that form; and in the absence of the
prophetic we are left with the merely political. There are
many fine, pungent and moving things in each of these
books, and Steinbeck has given *The Grapes of Wrath*
momentum, an inner drive, which in its generation only
Faulkner—and he only a few times—has equalled. It also

has a sweetness which never once goes sticky. Yet neither book quite touches bottom, quite manages to expose beneath the particular miseries and misfortunes the existence of what used to be called fate, what now is called the human condition—that twist or flaw in the very nature of things which Steinbeck has himself laid poetic hold of and expressed in the very similar phrases which conclude *The Red Pony* and *Of Mice and Men*, and which refer to two very similar acts of destruction: "I had to do it—had to" and "You hadda, George, I swear you hadda". *In Dubious Battle* and *The Grapes of Wrath* have, as it were, everything but that simple acknowledgment of the secret cause of our suffering and our violence. The secret cause is the ally of the poetic impulse, but these novels reach only as deep as the political cause, and politics in its usual meaning is the enemy of poetry, or anyhow of Steinbeck's poetry.

The Grapes of Wrath does not manage to transcend its political theme because the question "What is man?" was not really accepted by Steinbeck as the root question. He could not bring himself to believe that there was anything really wrong with the human heart, so that the causes of the wrongs observed must be other—practical, even mechanical; political, in short. The point here is that the application of Steinbeck's special and happy-natured poetry to his newly-discovered and unhappy historical materials could only result in a defeat of the poetry. It would have taken a different brand of poetry, something with a more tragic thrust to it, to have survived. *The Grapes of Wrath* remains with the political answer, the same political theme—unity—of *In Dubious Battle*, but what it does is to expand on that theme.

To the story of Tom Joad and his family—their long, rickety journey westward, their exhausted efforts to make a living in California, and the bitter resistance they encounter among the rich, frightened, and greedy land-owners—Steinbeck has added a large sky-blue vision of things which is not only like the vision of Emerson, it is straight out of Emerson. It is his notion of the over-soul, the world-soul of which each individual has his modest and particular share. Jim Casy, the former preacher and future martyr, pronounces this idea: "Maybe all men got one big soul and everybody's a part of it." He had come to this vision during his retirement into the hills: "There was the hills, an' there was me, an' we wasn't separate no more. We was one big thing. An' that one thing was holy. That's the Holy Spirit—the human spirit—the whole shebang. An' it on'y got unholy when one mis'able little fella got the bit in his teeth, an' run off his own way ... Fella like that bust the holiness."

The doctrine of the whole shebang is the warrant for all the desperate organisational efforts, the violence and the heroism which follow later; they are all efforts to reconstruct the busted holiness, to mend once more the unity of the one soul of mankind. That doctrine also is the philosophical basis for the famous speech that Tom Joad makes to his mother after Casy has been killed—those words which rang bravely and beautifully in 1939 but which, if you will forgive me, seem to have lost a little of their glow since. Tom Joad is about to leave, to continue the whole struggle in hiding. His mother asks: "How'm I gonna know about you? They might kill ya an' I wouldn' know."

"Tom laughed uneasily. 'Well, maybe like Casy says, a fella ain't got a soul of his own, but on'y a piece of a big one—an then . . . then it don't matter. Then I'll be all aroun' in the dark. I'll be ever'where—wherever you look. Wherever they's a fight so hungry people can eat. I'll be there. Wherever they's a cop beatin' up a guy, I'll be there. If Casy knowed, why, I'll be in the way guys yell when they're mad an'—I'll be in the way kids laugh when they're hungry an' they know supper's ready. An' when our folks eat the stuff they raise an' live in the houses they build—why, I'll be there. See?' "

What does get lost amidst the genuinely lyrical flow of that passage and in its infectious hopefulness is the element on which not only the social struggle but the art of narrative depend—the image of the sharply outlined, resolutely differentiated, concrete individual personality. The political movements of the 1930s did tend to submerge the individual in the group, whether or not at the behest of the over-soul, but in reflecting that fact in his fiction Steinbeck has again yielded up his poetry to his politics. And his poetry is not saved by adding above that political tendency a metaphysical principle which (even if true, as most probably it is not) is totally unsuited for the craft of fiction. Fiction deals with individuals, however intimately related. The relationship, in turn, which both fiction and politics were seeking, and are seeking, must be composed of inviolable and separate persons. A modern philosopher has wisely said that relationship depends upon distance. What seems to be needed, both for society and for art, is not unity, which dissolves the individuals within it, but community, which is a sharing among distinct human persons. What is needed is not group-men but companions. Steinbeck has always had trouble focusing on individuals, and he has always known it. "You have never known a person," Joseph Wayne's sister-in-law says to him; and we feel it is Steinbeck admonishing himself. "You aren't aware of persons, Joseph; only people. You can't see units, Joseph, only the whole." Therefore it is heartening as well as a trifle surprising to come at last and in *East of Eden* upon the long awaited awareness, the long delayed perception; to arrive in Steinbeck's pages at the revelation withheld from Joseph Wayne and even from Doc Burton and Jim Casy. And this occurs in a passage not wholly justified by the immediate context, but erupting with a fierceness of feeling reminiscent of the explosive and superficially irrelevant ode to democracy which pops up in the early pages of *Moby Dick*. "And this I believe," Steinbeck's voice suddenly announces to us: "And this I believe. That the free, exploring mind of the individual human is the most valuable thing in the world. And this I would fight for: the freedom of the mind to take any direction it wishes, undirected. And this I must fight against: an idea, religion or government which limits or destroys the individual. This is what I am and what I am about. I can understand why a system built on a pattern must try to destroy the free mind, for this is the one thing which can by inspection destroy such a system. Surely I can understand this, and I hate it and I will fight against it to preserve the one thing that separates us from the uncreative beasts. If the glory can be killed, we are lost."

It can no doubt be explained that such a belief and the passion behind it have been generated by revolt against the peculiar misbehaviours, the conformist pressures, of the 1950s, just as the emphasis on unity and the world-soul were stimulated by the ruggedly destructive individualism of the 1930s. But this time Steinbeck's rebellious impulse has produced a theme which goes beyond politics; which is, very simply and very greatly, human; which is the actual stuff of the art of narrative. *East of Eden* itself does not, as a novel, demonstrate this new and potentially happier wedding. But in the passage quoted Steinbeck's familiar daemon leapt out at us for an instant, and some day he will emerge to stay.

WILLIAM FAULKNER:
THE DOOMED AND THE DAMNED

BY CARLOS BAKER

THE YOUNG REBEL IN AMERICAN LITERATURE MAY BE an author or he may be a fictional character. If he is Henry Thoreau or Henry Mencken or Walt Whitman his voice is his own and he scorns ventriloquism. In this category of the young rebel, besides those who have been examined in the present series, one would place such men as Emerson, Jones Very, John Brown, Henry George, John Reed, or Vachel Lindsay—to name only a few in a country that has bred a great many. All of them have been strong and original personalities in revolt against the *status quo ante*. They have all demanded new styles in human architecture; they have all existed to correct, if they could, the spiritual astigmatism of their audiences; they were all young rebels and some were lucky enough to become old ones, too.

The second class of writers are not themselves necessarily young rebels, nor are they in the business of direct persuasion. They speak to us indirectly through the difficult medium of fiction; they offer us incarnations of the youthful spirit of rebellion. It may be young Carol Kennicott in revolt against the sour Gothic *mores* of a midwestern Main Street, or young Tom Joad in revolt against man's inhumanity to man among the green and golden gardens of California, or the great Gatsby in revolt against the values of an East Coast society by which he longs to be accepted.

The recurrent figure of the young rebel in Faulkner

has never had the attention he deserves. He appears again and again, a compulsively driven, almost obsessive figure who seldom understands the origin and meaning of his rebellious spirit, and would probably be too inarticulate to express these matters even if he understood them. His inward promptings often force him into lines of action which are not in strict accord with the prevailing customs of his social *milieu*. When this happens, he is victimised in some fashion. As a result the young rebel tends to stand apart, surrounded by suspicion, a cynosure of accusatory eyes. He is to an extraordinary degree the dupe-figure: dupe, that is, to a tragic or comic fortune whose causes may originate within himself (because he misreads the meaning of human life) or arise from social pressures (where others misread his rebellious intentions). Usually, of course, his fortune is the result of his own immense inward pressure thrusting against a social counter-pressure too huge and heavy to be finally withstood.

Robert Penn Warren is certainly correct in his view that the "constant ethical center of Faulkner's work is to be found in the glorification of the human effort and human endurance". If we use the remark as a diametric yardstick applied to Faulkner's young rebels, it is at once clear that while many of them exemplify the glories of the human effort and the powers of human endurance, there are others who are notably eccentric in these respects. Some are evidently intended to command our admiration while others are implicitly condemned, though not of course without sorrow and compassion that they are as they are.

It may be useful to distinguish two groups of young rebels in Faulkner as respectively the savers and the sinners. For there are those among them who by ancestry, birth, upbringing, or social habit are so constituted that they must try to save their fellow-men. There are also others who for various but always considerable reasons seem 'fated'—in a typical Faulknerian past participle—to be sinners, enemies of the people, peripheral outcasts. They torture themselves and others, or in turn are tortured by others. For our purposes it will be convenient to speak of the savers as the Doomed and the sinners as the Damned.

Although the distinction is mine, the words are Faulkner's. They ring throughout his work with something of the clangour of the death-bells in Poe's poem. Faulkner is not concerned to use them in any strict doctrinal sense, and would no doubt raise his eyebrows and spread his hands if he were asked to confirm the distinction. What he appears to mean is that there are people who seem to be doomed to save others: it is nothing less than their human lot. There are others, often but not invariably the 'victims' of social wrongs, who become destroyers—damning and damned. When Byron Bunch first saw the sign on the Reverend Gail Hightower's front lawn, he could not make out the meaning of the initials 'D.D.' which followed the name. His conclusion, deduced from the minister's evident failure as a social force, was that the letters stood for 'Done Damned'. Yet

Byron was mistaken. Despite his ineffectuality, Hightower is not a damned man, not a destroyer. He is only
a doomed man: doomed, that is, to save and serve his
fellow-mortals no matter how little they seem to want or
to deserve salvation.

The damned young rebels in Faulkner are not so
numerous as their counterparts in Dante, but they are not
hard to find. One is Jason Compson, the Fury of *The
Sound and the Fury*, who sees himself as the saviour of his
disintegrating family, the one fighting rebel capable of
standing up in valour against their moral and physical
dissolution, fleecing others of their golden fleece that the
façade of respectability may be maintained, yet destroy-
ing them, one after another, through the very fanaticism
of his preservational purpose. Jason is one of the damned.
So also, in a different way, is Darl, the poetic seer (one had
almost said *voyeur*) of *As I Lay Dying*. Unlike Jason, he
cares nothing for money; like Jason, he has a kind of
inward drive to torture other people. The physical
version of hell for him is the insane asylum at Jackson, and
it is a memorable fact that he goes there laughing.
Although he is evidently intended as a more sympathetic
character, Joe Christmas of *Light in August* is a young
rebel damned to die, as Faulkner rhetorically puts it, "in
the savage and lonely street which he had chosen of his
own will". He is the Cain-like outlaw. Faulkner's Paolo
and Francesca are the young Doctor Wilbourne and his
paramour Charlotte Rittenmeyer of *The Wild Palms*. To
them, as to Christmas, we shall have to return.

The most obviously damned among all Faulkner's

heroines is Temple Drake of *Sanctuary* and its sequel, *Requiem for a Nun*. As Temple is about to depart at the end of the latter book, she wonders half aloud whether there is anyone anywhere who can save her soul, and whether heaven, if it exists at all, is open to those who want salvation. "If there is none, I'm sunk," says Temple. "We all are. Doomed. Damned." The sequence of events from *Sanctuary* to *Requiem* (the religious terminology of the titles is worth noticing) clearly points to Temple as one of the damned. She has come to recognise her situation more and more plainly. She has a hunger for evil-doing that will stop neither at lying nor at murder. In her curtain line, she faces the fact: "I'm sunk ... I'm damned." Her capacity for evil-doing is not by any means absolute, as the nascent dawn of her contrition tends to indicate. Yet she knows its power is always likely to be too much for her to withstand.

Those who are doomed to serve and save constitute a fairly large group of people in Faulkner. Mr. Warren, in the essay already quoted, observes that Yoknapatawpha County contains its share of the 'good'. He names Byron Bunch, Lucas Beauchamp, Dilsey, Ike McCaslin, Uncle Gavin, Benbow, Ratliff, Hightower, and others. Among these we should certainly count the doomed young rebels. They invariably seek, as well as they can, to set all that right which has sagged awry.

Among them, at one extreme, would be the youthful idealists who wish to remake the world in the flickering light of their own sensibilities. Quentin Compson of *The Sound and the Fury* cannot endure the thought that his sister Caddy should be corrupted, and dies to keep alive the chivalric tradition which he refuses to see is already dead. The young aviator Levine of *A Fable* is the type of the aspiring spirit at war with itself, believing that he must die in order to convince himself and the world that life is better than death. The young Hightower, most thoroughgoing of unreconstructed dreamers while he occupies his pulpit, is doomed to age flabbily into the good man who can do nothing right, no matter how hard he tries, in a world he sees all wrong.

A far more effective group of savers and servers would include the young convict of the 'Old Man' sections of *The Wild Palms*; the fiercely heroic Jewel Bundren; young Chick Mallison of *Intruder in the Dust*; the 'nun', Nancy Mannigoe, of *Requiem*; and the anonymous illiterate corporal who succeeds temporarily in stopping the world war of *A Fable*. Whatever their religious professions, these people seem, in their youth and valour and endurance, to be the very types of the suffering servant ideal in the Hebraic-Christian tradition. At all events, as they learn and grow, it is towards this ideal that they seem to be moving.

An early and clear view of the doomed young rebel comes in the opening pages of *As I Lay Dying*. Two of the four sons of the dying Addie Bundren are walking home along a path through a cotton-field. Their names are Darl and Jewel. Darl is speaking. "Jewel and I come up from the field, following the path in single file. Although I am fifteen feet ahead of him, anyone watching us from the cotton-house can see Jewel's frayed and broken straw hat a full head above my own. The path runs straight as a plumbline, worn smooth by feet and baked brick-hard by July, between the green rows of laid-by cotton, to the cotton-house in the centre of the field, where it turns and circles the cotton-house at four soft right angles and goes on across the field again, worn so by feet in fading precision. The cotton-house is of rough logs. . . . Square, with a broken roof . . . it leans in empty and shimmering dilapidation in the sunlight, a single broad window in two opposite walls giving on to the approaches of the path. When we reach it I turn and follow the path where it circles the house. Jewel, fifteen feet behind me, looking straight ahead, steps in a single stride through the window. Still staring straight ahead, his pale eyes like wood set in his wooden face, he crosses the floor in four strides with the rigid gravity of a cigar-store Indian dressed in patched overalls and endued with life from the hips down, and steps in a single stride through the opposite window and into the path again as I come round the corner. In single file and five feet apart and Jewel now in front, we go on up the path toward the foot of the bluff."

Jewel is as typical of the young rebel in Faulkner as Byron's Manfred is typical of the Byronic hero. He is the spit and image of a dozen confrères who stride rigidly and furiously, with pale eyes, through the pages of Faulkner's novels. He is ordinarily grave and taciturn in manner. Whatever hopes he may nurture in that burning mind of his, he says nothing of them to anyone else. Instead he acts and endures. As Jewel scorns the 'soft corners' where the path turns round the cotton-house, choosing rather to pass in six unbroken strides through the near window, across the floor, and out through the far window, so the rebel in Faulkner is likely to move with ruthless driving power towards whatever goals he has chosen. We noticed that Darl's detour around two of the soft corners has lost him twenty paces. When Jewel emerges on the other side of the cotton-house, he is ahead of his brother, as he is also a head taller than his brother. The path, we have been told, runs as "straight as a plumbline". It is the essence of Jewel's character to move plumbline-straight, with a kind of fierce fanaticism and furious cold absorption, until he is within reach of or in possession of his object.

Jewel's taking the lead over his brother Darl at this point in the book is a prediction of things to come. For he will also take the lead over the whole family when they set out on their journey, the seemingly endless struggle to get Addie Bundren home for burial in the family plot at Jefferson. Jewel will literally bring his mother's body home to rest through flood and fire. The other members of the family will pursue their own devices under the disguise of a magnanimous and selfless series of actions. They will use the funeral journey as a means to ends other than the interment of the dead matriarch. Cash and Darl and their shiftless, self-pitying father Anse, along with Dewey Dell the pregnant but unmarried daughter and Vardaman the baffled little boy, form the members of the crew. But the directive brain belongs to Jewel. He is the unacknowledged legislator of their lives. He is the captain of all their souls because he is so unremittingly the captain of his own.

It is typical of Jewel, for example, that in the summer and autumn of his fifteenth year he should pursue a desired goal in secret and alone. His brothers begin to notice that each night he disappears, stays away all night, and returns about dawn to do, as well as he can, his own share of the family chores. He loses weight, looks drawn, and often falls asleep at the table even in the midst of the act of chewing. For five months, while his brothers specu-late with admiration on what they call the staying-powers of the woman they think he is visiting, these nocturnal activities continue. At last in November he comes riding home on a horse. He has earned it himself: the penniless fifteen-year-old boy, in order to own this something of his own, has succeeded in clearing forty acres of new planting-ground for a neighbouring farmer. He has worked all alone, at night, by the light of a lantern, asking no quarter from anyone, letting no one in on his secret. This horse, the symbol of Jewel's youthful rebelliousness, the living evidence of his refusal to stay shackled in the prison of his family's ignorance and shiftlessness, remains in Jewel's hands until the funeral journey is part-way through. Then Anse Bundren, epitome of shiftless ignor-ance, makes off with the horse, trading it towards the cost of a team of mules. It is typical of Jewel that he should accept the loss. It is now his fierce intention to get his mother's body to town and to grave. The horse must be sacrificed to that intention.

Like many of Faulkner's young rebels, Jewel stands apart. He is with the others but not of them. He is the one among the five children whose father was not Anse Bundren. He is the only child in the family actually conceived in love, though that love was adulterous. He is finally the single member of the family absolutely devoted to the fulfilment of his mother's dying wish to lie at home among her own people, who are not of the Bundren tribe any more than Jewel is. This angry, undeviating, and absolute devotion to a cause—like the quality of apartness, the fierce spiritual isolation, the gravity, the taciturnity, and the almost fanatical perseverance—is what stamps Jewel Bundren as the very type of the young rebel in Faulkner. He may look like one of the damned; he is really one of the doomed: those who are doomed to save and serve, though often in terms of their own choosing.

Chick Mallison, the hero of *Intruder in the Dust*, happens to be a young rebel who finds himself called on to serve and save in terms not strictly of his own choosing. Furthermore, though it takes him a whole book to learn it, he is in silent rebellion—like Huckleberry Finn—against the ancient tradition which says that a Negro must know his place and stay in it. But Chick must learn rebellion by having the need for it thrust upon him. Four years before the opening of the book, he tumbled into an icy creek near Lucas Beauchamp's house, and Lucas was there, huge above him on the wintry bank, to command him home to his kitchen to dry out and be fed. But the twelve-year-old boy could not be beholden to a Negro. He insisted on paying Lucas a seventy-cent fee for the drying and the dinner. Lucas refused. Young Chick hurled the coins to the cabin floor and shouted the command to Lucas—to pick them up. But the inflexible, intractable, proud old Negro would neither pick them up nor keep them, with the result that for years after the event of the icy creek, the boy would "writhe with impotent fury" at having been bested by a Negro in the game of saving face.

At sixteen, however, Chick is once more confronted with the game of saving face. This time it is Lucas's face which must be saved. And not only his face, his life as well. For a white man has been shot in the back, and Lucas has been found standing near the body holding a .41 Colt pistol from which one shot has been fired. Chick's problem is complicated by the old Negro's proud insistence on being human. But it is also complicated, for this boy who must accomplish the work of rescue, by a warfare within him between two opposed sets of values. One set pulls him back towards his twelve-year-old position: save face, keep the uppity Negro in his place. The other set, growing up within him almost instinctively, makes it impossible for him to bear the "injustice and outrage and dishonor and shame" that would ensue if he sat back and allowed Lucas Beauchamp to be lynched by a white mob from the hard-fisted Beat Four section of Yoknapatawpha County. It would be too much to say that young Chick Mallison gradually comes to embody the kind of thinking that must take place in the minds of Southern leaders in the next generation. It is certainly true that the context and the characters who contribute to Chick's struggle and to its moral outcome do make, together with that struggle, a deeply informed parable by a great Southern novelist about the land of his birth and upbringing.

The lawyer Gavin Stevens, thinking of men like Lucas Beauchamp, puts the matter well: "We—he and us—should confederate: swap him the rest of the economic and political and cultural privileges which are his right, for the reversion of his capacity to wait and endure and survive. Then we would prevail; together we would dominate the United States; we would present a front not only impregnable but not even to be threatened by a mass of people who no longer have anything in common save a frantic greed for money and a basic fear of a failure of national character which they hide from one another behind a loud lipservice to a flag." As in the boy Chick Mallison, there is that in the moral structure of the South against which it will have to rebel if the new confederation is to prevail—just as there is also in the South, as in this young rebel, a growing hatred towards injustice, outrage, dishonour, and shame which it has hitherto tolerated but will not tolerate much longer.

If the great outward enemy is materialistic greed, the great inward enemy is fear. Joe Christmas, the *mulatto agonistes* of *Light in August*, both embodies and elicits the enmity of fear. He is one of the damned in Faulkner: like Lucas Beauchamp in his stubborn pride, yet the very antithesis of Lucas Beauchamp in that the unhappy circumstances of his birth and upbringing have burned the humanity out of him as by the cautery of fire. We have not gone beyond the thirty-third page of *Light in August* when we come upon two figures working side by side at a sawdust pile in a Mississippi planing-mill. One is a weak-faced young Judas-figure, betrayer of a country girl named Lena Grove. Except to notice that Faulkner manages to make him at once into a Judas and a comic character, this young man need not concern us here. Beside him is another man, "ruthless, lonely, and proud", with a "dark insufferable face" on which he does not attempt to disguise the look of "cold and quiet contempt" which he feels for his companion and his surroundings. There is, Faulkner tells us, "something definitely rootless about him, as though no town nor city was his, no street, no walls, no square of earth his home". A cigarette pulls down one corner of his mouth, and through its rising smoke his face looks out expressionlessly—"darkly and contemptuously still". Faulkner's modifiers signal: this is another of his young rebels. His name is Joe Christmas, and the greater part of *Light in August* is his personal biography.

Christmas is one of the damned, marked early as a member of the outcast tribe of Cain. Abandoned on Christmas night on the doorstep of a house of ill-fame in Memphis, he was named by the ladies within the house in raucous parody of the feast-day and the name of Joseph. Christmas is the fruit of a union between a white girl and a coloured man, and the blood of the two races —running at cross-purposes—constitutes the very cross upon which he is inwardly crucified, chiefly by himself.

157

His story is not so much a story of miscegenation as a story of the tragic consequences of miscegenation in the mind of one of its offspring.

So far as his material permitted, Faulkner was at pains to suggest rough and even rude parallels between the life of Our Lord, an early victim of a lynching, and the life of this young latter-day rebel who in the thirty-third year of his life is shot to death and mutilated in the kitchen of a minister's house in Jefferson, Mississippi. Faulkner follows his parallel along the sinister side of parody—the name, the age, the week-end of the passion, and so on. In Joe's ruthless treatment of the woman who befriends him there is more than a suggestion of the "Woman, what have I to do with thee?" of the Gospel story. There is a hint of the lance in the side when the military young man named Percy Grimm ruthlessly lacerates Christmas with a butcher-knife as he lies near death from previous wounds. And in the Faulknerian rhetoric which brings Joe's story to a close one even catches a hint of the idea of resurrection.

Joe's personal insurrection is chiefly induced by a society which fears him and can find no place in which to accommodate him. He rebels fiercely against the legalistic fundamentalism of that neo-Pharisee, his foster-father McEachern. But he turns with even greater ferocity against the white woman Joanna Burden, whose whole life has been devoted to the gradual cultural rehabilitation of the Negro in the South until Joe first corrupts, then exploits, and finally murders her in cold blood. Despite the ironic Christian parallels, Joe emerges as a social outcast, a self-condemned outlaw, and finally as a kind of dark Antichrist. That the mark is upon him is at least suggested strongly when he breaks in upon the revival meeting in a Negro church twenty miles out of Jefferson. As he pushes the preacher from his pulpit and climbs into his place to hurl obscene imprecations against God, he is probably rightly identified by the hysterical woman who screams: "It's the Devil! It's Satan himself." As victim of an intolerant society, Joe Christmas can be pitied in the words of the preacher Hightower, who cries, "Poor man. Poor mankind," in something of the true Christian spirit. But as the dark, savage, almost Byronic figure in rebellion and revolt, he seems satanic—cast out, as it were, by the logic of his own contempt.

It is one of the hallmarks of Faulkner's fiction, though none of his critics has adequately shown it, that he is able to make the tragic and the comic operate in a kind of friendly colloquium. Although *Light in August* is mostly the book of Joe Christmas, its leitmotif is provided by the essentially comic story of Byron Bunch. Byron is the least Byronic of creatures, assuredly no rebel, yet not an oaf. It is his doom, which he seems to enjoy, to be the good young man devoted to serving and saving, sweeping up the loose carbon from the streets after the dark, fire-breathing dragons have passed by. His courtship of Lena Grove, like his quixotic pursuit of her faithless lover Lucas Burch, is a touching human comedy to set beside the tragic story of Joe Christmas.

The critical recognition of this habit of Faulkner's throws some light into the dark corners of his intention in *The Wild Palms,* the generic title for a set of two inter-woven *novellae,* one mainly in the tragic mode, and the other chiefly in the comic mode. The tragic story traces the declining fortunes of Charlotte Rittenmeyer and Harry Wilbourne after they have run away together, she from her marriage and he from his profession. The comic story, which is not without its heroic moments, examines the adventures of a young convict in rescuing a mother and child during the great flood on the Mississippi River in the spring of 1927.

So far as I know, no really satisfactory explanation has been offered as to why Faulkner chose to interweave these two stories. Yet it is clear, following the lines of our present investigation, that both these young men—to say nothing of the fiercely emancipated Mrs. Rittenmeyer—are rebels. The convict is one doomed to save and serve, though ruefully and perhaps even sardonically. Dr. Harry Wilbourne is damned by his own pseudo-romantic beliefs into a social isolation not unlike that of Joe Christmas. Both young men, furthermore, have been betrayed by women and by their own masculine imaginations into lawless rebellion against certain of the rules of society.

Nor are these the only connections between the convict and the doctor. They likewise share the predicament which the Reverend Gail Hightower once expressed: "How false the most profound book turns out to be when applied to life." The flaw in their thinking has been precisely this, that they have sought to apply bookish notions to the act of living, even though the books from which they derived their ideas could scarcely be called very profound. The convict's taste in literature did not transcend paper-back dime novels about Diamond Dick and Jesse James, along with some sensational material from a sheet called the *Detectives' Gazette*. The doctor's taste ran to ecstatic poetry by certain of the more romantic female poets who wrote in the 1920s and the early 1930s.

Our first view of the convict reveals the familiar outlines of the young Faulknerian rebel. He is "about twenty-five, tall, lean, flat-stomached, with a sunburned face and Indian-black hair and pale, china-colored outraged eyes". The outrage in his eyes is against the writers of cheap fiction about notorious American bad-men, for these anonymous *littérateurs* have led him to think that it is not only possible but even admirable to bring off an armed train robbery without getting caught and going to prison for it. He is rather less than half-way through with a fifteen-year prison sentence, and his impotent rage is, if anything, increasing with the passage of time. So, as Faulkner puts it, whenever the convict "trod the richly shearing black earth behind his plough or with a hoe thinned the sprouting cotton and corn or lay on his sullen back in his bunk after supper, he cursed in a harsh steady unrepetitive stream" against the anonymous ghost-writers who had deceived him into the Mississippi State Penal Farm. He is perhaps too natively chivalrous to curse his boyhood sweetheart, a short-legged, big-breasted girl with a "heavy mouth and dull eyes like ripe muscadines, who owned a baking-powder can almost full of ear-rings and brooches and rings bought (or presented at suggestion) from ten-cent stores". She is now, for her sins, the fattening bride of a Mr. Vernon Waldrip. As he drives his plough or dreams in his bunk, the young convict half suspects that it was for the dubious rewards half-promised by the muscadine girl with the ten-cent jewellery that he tried to rob the train in dubious imitation of his dime-novel Jesse Jameses and Diamond Dicks. Yet it is probably because he is so well 'cured' of both women and literature that he is capable of turning in, as if it were a mere day's work, a performance of almost superhuman devotion and heroism in the rescue of a mother and child from the floodwaters.

Dr. Harry Wilbourne, the tragic rebel of the other novelette, is on the whole less interesting than his comic counterpart. He is an intern in a New Orleans hospital who almost inadvertently finds himself eloping with a married woman less than two months after they have first met at a cocktail party. He, too, is victimised by a romantic dream which he defines as "the passionate idea of two [people in love] damned and doomed and isolated for ever against the world and God". For this he sacrifices the life of his paramour and his own career in medicine: when she becomes pregnant, he uses his medical knowledge, at her insistence, to interrupt the pregnancy, and she dies of the ensuing infection. All this is stark enough, but young Dr. Wilbourne prefers to romanticise his love affair, talking and thinking about it in what one of his friends scornfully calls "ninth-rate [Sara] Teasdale". For where the convict has read Jesse James, Wilbourne has bitten off more fusty-gusty poetical gumbo than he can chew. Even in the end, standing in his prison cell and holding in his hand the melodramatic pellet of cyanide which his girl's husband has given him, he sticks to his dream. His closing soliloquy centres on the old question of "to be or not to be". He decides in the end that even a life filled with the smart and agony of an unstillable remorse is preferable to the painless nihilism of death. "Between grief and nothing," as he quietly sums it up, "I will take grief." If his story has an aspect of comic irony, it is that young Dr. Wilbourne never managed to read the story of the convict in floodtime: the laconic young train-robber might presently have divested him of some of his more withering self-deceptions.

Faulkner's interest in human demonology and incipient social sainthood bulk large in his recent work. *Requiem for a Nun* depends for much of its effect on the striking confrontation of the damned by the doomed. In *Sanctuary*, Temple Drake was imprisoned in a Memphis bawdy-house as the aftermath to a college week-end party. Her escort, a young weakling named Gowan Stevens, became drunk, wrecked an automobile, and passed out, leaving Temple to the questionable mercies of a degenerate Italian gangster named Pop-eye. In the sequel this same Temple Drake, now married to Gowan and the mother of his two children, is in process of developing to their logical conclusion those impulses towards evil-doing which her experience in Memphis long ago made manifest to her. Her drive towards damnation is accelerated by the attraction she feels for another Memphis gangster named Pete, with whom she is on the point of running away.

Pete looks and acts like the damned young rebel. "There is a definite 'untamed' air to him," writes Faulkner. "He is handsome, attractive to women, not at all unpredictable because you . . . know exactly what he will do, you just hope he won't do it this time. He has a hard, ruthless quality." His search for money in Temple's rooms is conducted "thoroughly and savagely" and "with a sort of bleak and contemptuous disgust". Like a magnet he draws Temple towards his own way of life. She is ready to leave her husband, ready even, at least in her heart, to murder her younger child, in order to secure Pete's affection. The very least of her sacrificial offerings seems to her a coloured woman named Nancy Mannigoe, whom she had known in the old days in Memphis and has since picked up, almost literally off the streets, to serve as 'nanny' for her children, the boy named Bucky and the murdered baby.

Confronting Temple and the gangster in the crucial episode of this terrifying story is the oddly saint-like figure of Nancy Mannigoe herself. She is a much-manhandled waif, completely uneducated except in the ways of the lower depths of human society. Yet, by a kind of longing reversal of all the horrors she has known, Nancy is determined if she can to keep the Stevens family together. It is not through admiration for Gowan Stevens, nor yet through any but the most rudimentary liking for Temple. It is simply, if possible, that she wishes to save the House of Stevens for the sake of the small, surviving child Bucky. To make this possible, she has taken the full blame for the baby's murder and mutely accepted the sentence of death.

At the last minute, having returned from vacation in California with the shreds of her tattered conscience, Temple goes with her lawyer Gavin Stevens to see the governor of the State, in the remote expectation of getting Nancy pardoned. It is, of course, too late. But the governor himself, while not fully aware of the facts of the case, is able to sense the incipient sainthood of Nancy Mannigoe. He recognises her as one of those rebels-against-the-nature-of-things who are doomed to serve and save, even to the point of actual martyrdom. He appreciates the human worth of Nancy's "simple, undeviable aim", which is to die in order to shield the child Bucky from the terrors of a broken and motherless house. "Who am I," asks the governor, "to have the brazen temerity and hardihood to set the puny appanage of my office in the balance against that simple undeviable aim? Who am I to render null and abrogate the purchase she made with that poor crazed lost and worthless life?" He will not save Nancy from the gallows because he sees that if she dies for a cause—a cause which amounts to nothing less than love—she can redeem a life which has otherwise been worse than worthless.

The lawyer Gavin Stevens formulates the cause in words that Nancy, ignorant and inarticulate as she is, could never summon up. She will die, he says, for the principle that "little children, as long as they are little

children, shall be intact, unanguished, untorn, unterri-
fied". Even though Nancy Mannigoe could never put it
so, this is her basic ethical postulate, the conviction she
dies to establish. Having led a life beyond the pale, she
has none the less caught a glimpse of a moral value beyond
the grasp of her alleged superiors. Nancy Mannigoe is in
rebellion against all that has made her life what it has been
up to the point of her dying. She is the type of the rebel
as saint.

Faulkner's interest in the rebelliousness of sainthood
continues in *A Fable*, that astonishing *tour de force* which
seems to have tipped the balance in his favour in the
award of the Nobel Prize for Literature. Of all the young
rebels in Faulkner, the illiterate, thirty-three-year-old
corporal who succeeds in bringing the First World War
to a temporary halt is surely the crowning instance of the
young rebel doomed to serve and save in order that
others may see, and perhaps understand, the ethical
values he exists to demonstrate. For *A Fable* takes as its
theme the impingement of an absolute standard of moral
conduct on a human society which is relativistic in its
ethical orientation. Faulkner once again develops, as he
had done very darkly in the story of Joe Christmas, a
continuous parallel between the birth, ministry, death,
and resurrection of Jesus Christ and a modern instance of
martyrdom. The ingenuity with which he manipulates
his parallels is, in both cases, worthy of notice. Yet the
real point of *A Fable* does not so much lie in the parallels
as grow out of them. For Faulkner is interested in showing us what happens when an almost impossible ethical

166

ideal is applied to human society—becomes genuinely active in its midst—at any time in history. The point in time is in fact unimportant, for the absolute is always potentially present, and it may bisect the actual at any moment when a human vehicle or agency sufficiently recognises it.

The story of *A Fable* is that of the mutiny of a French regiment in the trenches one Monday night in May 1918. They simply refuse to attack the enemy. How this situation came about, how it developed and gained momentum until the whole war was temporarily stopped, and what its aftermath was—these are the phases of Faulkner's fable. The book opens on a Wednesday morning after the mutiny of Monday night. In a large French city a huge crowd has gathered to watch the arrival of a fleet of army trucks bearing the three thousand mutineers. One vehicle contains the corporal and his twelve squad members, the rough modern equivalents of Jesus and his disciples. The mutiny is traceable to these thirteen. For more than a year, the corporal has been known to all combat troops below the rank of sergeant. He is not so much known as a man as he is felt as a force: a serving and saving force designed to convert all the young men into rebels.

In one conversation a pair of soldiers are discussing him. One says to the other: "You don't need to understand. Just go and look at him." The other: "Him? So it's just one, now?" And the first answers: "Wasn't one enough to tell us the same thing all them 2,000 years ago: that all we ever needed to do was just to say, Enough of this—us, not even the sergeants and the corporals, but just us, all of us, Germans and Colonials and Frenchmen and all the other foreigners in the mud here, saying together: Enough. Let them that's already dead and maimed and missing be enough of this—a thing so easy and simple that even human man, as full of evil and sin and folly as he is, can understand and believe it this time. Go on and look at him." Throughout the novel, this is what people of various ranks and statures actually do, and to this experience they react according to their several natures. Even after his execution, the young rebel remains as an influence—the absolute of Christian love, visible as a beacon if unattainable as a goal.

The degree to which this beacon is visible is perhaps the ultimate distinction between the two sets of young rebels in Faulkner. The company of the damned display our common, self-generated, self-blinding predilection for "evil and sin and folly". Temple Drake, Charlotte Rittenmeyer, Joe Christmas, Harry Wilbourne, Jason Compson, young Bayard Sartoris in the novel that bears his name, and even Labove, the football player of *The Hamlet*, all show, in their several ways, the prevalence of selfhood in the human race. The doomed young rebels, on the contrary, the savers and the servers, repeatedly prove through vision and action that we are neither necessarily damned, as Temple Drake seems to suppose, nor are we incapable of choosing good. By such a company as Jewel Bundren and Nancy Mannigoe and Chick Mallison, the young convict of the flooded river and the young corporal of *A Fable*, we are powerfully reminded of the immanent presence of grace. Such young rebels as these support Faulkner's belief, set forth in his speech of acceptance of the Nobel Prize in Literature, that man need not merely endure, he may ultimately prevail over the propensity to evil and sin and folly that is part of his human heritage.

NOTES ON LECTURERS

CARL BODE

Professor of English at the University of Maryland; on leave as Cultural Attaché, American Embassy, London. He is the editor of Thoreau's poems, co-editor of his letters, and author of two books on the cultural history of Thoreau's time, *The American Lyceum: Town Meeting of the Mind* and *An Anatomy of American Popular Culture 1840–61.*

DAVID DAICHES

University Lecturer in English and Fellow of Jesus College, Cambridge; formerly Professor of English and Chairman of the Division of Literature, Cornell University. He is the author of several books concerned wholly or in part with American literature.

GEOFFREY MOORE

Lecturer in American Literature at the University of Manchester; he taught previously at the Universities of Wisconsin and Kansas. His most recent work is the British Council pamphlet *Poetry To-Day.*

WALTER BEZANSON

Associate Professor of American Civilization at Rutgers University. He is the editor of Herman Melville's *Clarel* and the author of critical essays in the field of American fiction.

LEWIS LEARY

Professor of English at Columbia University. Formerly managing editor of *American Literature,* he is the author of books on colonial literary figures as well as of articles on nineteenth- and twentieth-century American writers.

R. W. B. LEWIS

Professor of English at Rutgers University. He is the author of *The American Adam* and *The Picaresque Saint,* a study of modern fiction in Europe and America. He also contributes to American literary periodicals. He has received several awards for his work.

CARLOS BAKER

Woodrow Wilson Professor of Literature at Princeton University. He is the author of several studies on the nineteenth-century English Romantics as well as of *Hemingway: The Writer as Artist* and the novel *A Friend in Power.*